PROJECT 2019

Socioeconomic Equality
Through Formal Education

6 - 12 - 2005

Thank you for your support.

By Charles E. Sanford

Published by Hundred Schools Publishing, USA

ISBN 0-9669834-1-6

Library of Congress Catalog Card Number: 99-90407

Web Site   http://www.project2019.com
E-Mail Address   ChuckSanford@prodigy.net

PREFACE

The widespread mayhem and the senseless violence of the 1992 Los Angeles riots inspired me to write a five-page manifesto entitled "Project 2012." It was the blueprint for what would become Project 2019. Like Project 2019, "Project 2012" called for a twenty-year plan for the socioeconomic advancement of black America. Like Project 2019, "Project 2012" was based on straightforward logic and empirical evidence that black America cannot attain socioeconomic equality with white America until it reaches educational equivalency with white America.

Of course, the seeds for Project 2019 were sown long before the 1992 acquittals of the police officers in the first Rodney King trial. In the 1950's, my mother was a single parent who often worked two jobs in order to support herself and her six children. Yet, she took the time and found the energy to teach her children all the important lessons that would be necessary to sustain them in the coming years. And, although she had very little formal education, one of the most valuable lessons that my mother taught her children was that education and knowledge are the keys to success in America.

PREFACE

My mother did not engage her children in deep, philosophical discussions about the meaning or nature of knowledge. There were only the lectures and the daily reminders that getting a good education had to be our number one priority. This mantra was reinforced by her unwavering insistence that, in spite of what we might think, she knew what was best for her children.

Looking back to my teenage years, it is now obvious that I listened to and took to heart the lessons my mother was teaching. It is now clear why my four best friends were who they were and why we gravitated towards each other. And it is not at all surprising that we all managed to earn at least one college degree and now all have successful, productive lives.

In spite of the hazards and perils of growing up on the West Side of Chicago, my siblings and I managed to avoid the pitfalls that often snare undisciplined and undirected youths. We attended college, developed careers, and we all have productive, happy lives. My eldest sister was a lab technician and my older brother is a successful attorney. One of my younger sisters is a school principal, another is a manager, and the youngest works at my alma mater, the University of Illinois, Chicago.

My mother's passion for education and knowledge has also been passed down to the next generation of her family. Of her nine adult grandchildren, six have already earned at least one college degree and a seventh is a college freshman. One grandchild has just completed

PREFACE

law school and another, my daughter, will become the first doctor in the family when she receives her doctorate in psychology in the year 2000.

My mother has always been one of the most intelligent and pragmatic persons that I have known. She was wise enough to understand that if being hardworking, ambitious, and smart were good then being those things and having a college degree was even better. Considering her lack of formal education and her having grown up in the South during the Jim Crow era, what she has accomplished through her family is remarkable. She is a remarkable black woman. She, however, is not alone.

There are, in fact, millions of remarkable black mothers and black fathers in America. Unfortunately, because black America is working from such a distinct disadvantage, there are not enough of them. And just as it takes a village to raise a child, it will take all of black America's remarkable mothers and fathers working in concert if we are to ever elevate the educational level of black America. All of black America's remarkable mothers and fathers must go beyond convincing their own children of the importance of education. They must help to convince all of black America's children that in the twenty-first century there will be no viable substitute for knowledge.

The message of Project 2019 is that "knowledge is power." It is a message that all black children need to hear, to understand, and to believe. We, the current

PREFACE

generation of black Americans, must ensure that this message is delivered. It is the debt that we owe to those who gave all that they had and all that they were to bring us to the gates of the Promised Land. We must ensure that the next generation of black Americans finally passes through those gates. We owe no less to our children, our grandchildren, and all future generations of black Americans.

CONTENTS

THE MISSION OF PROJECT 2019

PROJECT 2019 ISSUES

<u>PROJECT 2019 HEROES</u>

PROJECT 2019

THE MISSION

Mission Statement

Mission
The mission of Project 2019 is to elevate the socioeconomic status of black America.

Major Goal
The major goal of Project 2019 is to increase the level of formal education attained by black Americans to the same level of formal education attained by white Americans.

Primary Objectives
The primary objectives of Project 2019 are:
(1) To convince black America to embrace the truism "knowledge is power."
(2) To convince black America that the best way to acquire knowledge is through formal education.
(3) To motivate black America to increase the level of formal education attained by black Americans.

Measurement

The measurement of the success of Project 2019 will be the percentage of black Americans who earn college degrees versus the percentage of white Americans who earn college degrees.

Completion Date

The completion date for Project 2019 is the year 2019.

Basis For The Mission

The Mission Of Project 2019

American history can be a source of confusion if one believes that the United States was founded on such lofty principles and high ideals as "freedom, equality and justice for all." To eliminate most of the confusion, simply replace "all" with "all white, Anglo-Saxon, Protestant males." For many Americans, freedom, equality, and justice were not guaranteed. In the case of black Americans, freedom, equality, and justice were prohibited by law and tradition. It has taken almost four centuries but America has finally evolved to the point where "freedom, equality, and justice for all" does include "all" citizens of the United States.

During the three hundred and eighty years it has taken for this evolution to occur, black America has had three great missions. The first mission was to end the barbaric horror of Slavery. The second was to end the injustice and oppression of the Jim Crow era. Black America's third and hopefully its last great mission is to end the socioeconomic inequality that has resulted from Slavery and the Jim Crow era.

The Goals and Objectives Of Project 2019

The basis for Project 2019 is the certainty that black America will never attain socioeconomic equality with white America until it achieves educational equivalency with white America. For three and a half centuries, racism was the underlying reason for the lack of success of most black Americans. This began to change when black America entered the Equal Opportunity era three decades ago.

As America enters the twenty-first century, racism, sexism, and religious and ethnic discrimination continue to decline. These tools of oppression are becoming less and less powerful against minorities that were once easily disenfranchised by their power. In the new millenium, the success or failure of all of America's citizens will increasingly be determined by their education and knowledge rather than by their gender or the color of their skin.

While this may be good news for black Americans, the bad news is that white America is much better educated than black America. Twenty-four percent of white Americans have completed at least four years of college versus thirteen percent of black Americans. White America is therefore in a better position to meet the demands and reap the rewards of the age of technology. The major goal of Project 2019 is to ensure that black America is equally prepared for the challenges of the twenty-first century and beyond.

In order for black America to reach the goal of educational equivalency with white America, black America must accept and embrace the truism "knowledge is power." Black America must recognize and accept that the best way to acquire knowledge is through formal education. And, finally, black America must be inspired and motivated to reach educational equivalency, by any means necessary.

College Degrees As A Measurement

The measurement of the success of Project 2019 is limited to formal education attained, specifically higher education. Project 2019 does not directly address entrepreneurship or trade or vocational training. This is not because the value of such efforts are not recognized or equally regarded. They are not addressed because a focused, laser approach is necessary to make significant gains in any of these areas. Even so, a major success in any one of these areas would make it easier for black America to achieve success in each of the other areas.

Project 2019 does not include measurable objectives for primary or secondary formal education attained or any qualitative measurements of academic achievement. While these elements are critical for the success of Project 2019, it is not necessary to make them measurable objectives considering the one measurement that is driving the major goal. That is, it is not possible to double the number of black Americans who earn college degrees without a substantial increase in the number of high school graduates. Nor is it possible to double the number of blacks who earn college degrees without a significant improvement in the overall academic achievement of black Americans.

The measurement to be used to establish, track, and to determine the success of Project 2019 must remain straightforward and finite. It is based on the percentages of bachelor's degrees, master's degrees, doctoral degrees, law degrees, medical degrees, etc., earned by white Americans versus black Americans.

The Year 2019 Completion Date

The roots of Slavery can be traced to the selling of twenty black indentured servants to the inhabitants of the Jamestown Colony in 1619. Therefore, the year 2019 will be the four hundredth anniversary of the beginning of Slavery in America. With the success of Project 2019, this anniversary can be celebrated as a watershed moment in black America's history. It would be the first time that black Americans are full and equal partners in pursuit of the American dream. It would also be a fitting tribute to the millions who sacrificed their labor and their lives to make freedom and equality a reality for their descendants.

The year 2019 is twenty years, one generation, away. To some, a generation may seem to be an unnecessarily long time to complete Project 2019. To others, twenty years may not seem to be enough time for such a monumental undertaking. There is also the consideration that the amount of time it takes to complete a task expands or contracts to meet the due date assigned to it.

Twenty years, one generation, is a reasonable time frame for black America to reach educational equivalency with white America. If this time frame is a little short, it only means that black Americans will have to work harder to reach the goal. If it is a little long, then the bar can be raised by setting new goals and establishing new objectives.

The year 2019 will be one of the most notable years in the history of black America. However, if 2019 is to be one of the most successful years in the history of black America, it must be the result of thousands of successful days. A successful day is each day that a black American realizes the importance of Project 2019 and understands the reasons why it must succeed. A successful day is each day that a black American resolves to do his or her part to help ensure the success of the next generation and all future generations of black Americans.

PROJECT 2019

ISSUES

Regarding The Issues

Although the "Issues" presented in this publication are obviously related and certainly connected, they are, for the most part, presented as individual and complete discussions. This approach was taken so that as little as possible would be lost if the Issues were not read in sequence or if a reader chose to focus on any one Issue or on a selected group of Issues. This approach was also taken in anticipation of future publications of *"Project 2019"* in which issues will be presented and discussed by multiple authors.

There are many issues that will impact the nature and the progress of Project 2019. Clearly, no one person knows all the questions. Certainly, no one person has all the answers. If Project 2019 is to succeed, there must be a cooperative effort to determine the most pertinent and the most critical issues. There must then be open and meaningful dialog regarding these issues and the merits of the associated arguments and proposals. This process will best ensure the continued progress and the eventual success of Project 2019.

The Creation And History Of Black America

In the autumn of 1967, President Lyndon Johnson appointed a commission of political, business, and civil rights leaders to investigate the inner city rioting that had occurred in the summer of that year. The commission, chaired by Illinois Governor Otto Kerner, concluded in its 1968 report that the riots were the results of white racism and enduring economic inequality. The Kerner Commission also issued its often-quoted warning:

"Our nation is moving toward two societies, one black, one white – separate and unequal."

While this ominous warning by the Kerner Commission was accurate, unfortunately, it was issued three and a half centuries after the fact. The warning came too late to prevent the rape of a continent and the deaths of millions of innocent African men, women, and children. The warning came too late to prevent the enslavement of millions of black Americans for almost two and half centuries. The warning came to late to prevent hundreds of years of race related violence, including millions of slave beatings, thousands of slave revolts, the American Civil War and, of course, the inner city riots of 1967.

The Creation Of Black America

Thousands of years before Africans were brought to America, cultivation and other civilizing factors ended the nomadic existence of humankind. Human societies quickly progressed from homogeneous tribal units and villages to the first large nation-states and empires. This was the beginning of ethnic minorities – groups of people who differ in race or color or in national, religious, or cultural origin from the dominant group. The fate of ethnic minorities has ranged from acceptance and assimilation to complete domination and enslavement.

Given the turbulent and aggressive history of humans and their penchant for war and conquest, nations with ethnic minorities have been the rule. A notable modern day exception is Japan where the ethnic majority includes ninety-nine percent of the population. At the other end of the spectrum is the United States. From the homogeneity that existed at the time of the original thirteen colonies, America has become a country where nationality is now hyphenated with pride. Americans choose not to simply be Americans, instead they proclaim themselves to be Anglo-American, Italian-American, German-American, Russian-American, African-American, and so forth.

This is not to suggest that America's reputation as being the great "melting pot" is not deserved. Although, historically, new immigrants faced some resentment by those who felt most threatened by their arrival, within a generation or less they found their way and found a place in America. And considering the many nationalities, cultures, and religions that comprise the American people, America is a model of success in "same-race" ethnic mixing.

The reason for the "same-race" caveat is that America has never defined ethnic minorities based on "race or color or national, religious, or cultural origin." In America, ethnic minorities have always been distinguished and defined, first and foremost, based on "race and color." "National, religious, or cultural origin" has always been a secondary distinction of ethnicity in America. This is the reason why white South Africans who migrate to America do not consider themselves to be African-Americans. And it is the reason why blacks who migrate from England to America are not considered to be Anglo-Americans.

It was evident from the beginning that the black race would be a distinct and separate entity in America. In 1619, the year before the Mayflower brought the Pilgrims to Plymouth Rock, the first blacks were sold as "indentured servants" by a Dutch captain to settlers at Jamestown. Jamestown, the first permanent English settlement in North America, had been established only a decade earlier in 1607.

While there are no historical records that document the fate of these first black Americans, there is also little reason to believe that they, unlike white indentured servants, ever regained their freedom. In any case, based on various rationales, including racial, financial, religious, and even John Locke's "Fundamental Constitutions," within the next few decades, the institution of chattel slavery was firmly established in America. By the end of the century, tens of thousands of Africans were being brought to America annually and being sold into Slavery.

Although black America's history begins in 1619, more than a century and a half before the founding of the United States, black America was implicitly established on June 21, 1788. On that day, New Hampshire became the ninth state to ratify the United States Constitution, making it the supreme law of the land. Article 1, Section 2 of the Constitution detailed the manner in which House of Representative members would be elected based on state population. It is here that the Constitution declares that each slave was to be counted as "three-fifths" of a whole person. If there was any doubt that black America was and would continue to be a separate and distinct entity within America, this constitutional distinction erased that doubt.

Project 2019 divides black America's history into three major eras:

Slavery Era   1619-1865
The Slavery era spanned two hundred and forty-six years. It began with the arrival of the first black slaves in

America and ended with the ratification of the 13th Amendment to the Constitution, which officially abolished Slavery. During the Slavery era, millions of Africans were brought to America where they lived as slaves and died as slaves. Also, during the Slavery era, millions of black Americans were born, lived their lives, and died as slaves.

For the thousands of free black Americans who lived during this era, their lives were infinitely better than the lives of slaves. Even so, the lives of most free black Americans were austere, constrained, and precarious. Living in a country that was racist at its core, they were denied the vote by most Northern states and, in general, they had the protection of law only in the most obvious and extreme cases of injustice. Opportunities for most free black Americans generally included only menial jobs or manual labor. All lived their lives hearing tales of free black Americans being kidnapped and sold into Slavery in the Deep South.

Jim Crow Era   1866-1968

The Jim Crow era of black America's history endured for one hundred and three years. This era began with the Reconstruction legislation that was suppose to give black Americans equal access, equal rights, and equal protection under the law and it ended with the civil rights legislation of the 1960's that finally did. In addition to the Civil Rights Act of 1968, 1968 was also the year Martin Luther King was assassinated. It was his death and the events that followed that finally delivered black America to the gates of the Promised Land.

During the Jim Crow era, black America was as much of a distinct and separate entity within America as it had been during the Slavery era. In the South, segregation and exclusion were legislated or accomplished by intimidation or violence. In many ways, the lives of black Americans were no better than they had been for free blacks during the Slavery era. In the North, segregation and exclusion typically were not legislated. However, institutionalized racism severely limited the civil rights of black Americans and greatly reduced their opportunities for success.

Equal Opportunity Era   1969-Present

The Equal Opportunity era began in 1969 and, to date, has lasted thirty years. The era began after the passage of the Civil Rights Act of 1968. This was the final piece of civil rights legislation that, along with a series of court cases, established and guaranteed equal access, equal rights, and equal protection under the law for black Americans.

In the Equal Opportunity era, racism continues to be a factor in America. However, civil rights laws are now almost universally enforced and black Americans can remedy illegal racial discrimination when it is encountered. And although black Americans are starting from a distinct disadvantage, they now have the best opportunity in their history to be successful in America.

24

The constitutional distinction that separated black America from the rest of America ended in 1868 with the ratification of the 14th Amendment. This amendment, which made former slaves citizens, declares that black Americans were to be counted as whole persons rather than three-fifths of a person. The legal distinction of Jim Crow era laws that separated black America from the rest of America ended with the *BROWN V. BOARD OF EDUCATION OF TOPEKA, KANSAS* Supreme Court decision of 1954. However, black America as a separate and distinct entity within America still exists and for a number of reasons will continue to exist.

The Proud History And Future Of Black America

At this point in its history, black America must deal with the residual effects of the Slavery era and the Jim Crow era. After all, these two eras comprise ninety-two percent of black America's history and it is not a simple matter to reverse the results of three and a half centuries of oppression. What is needed is an immense sense of unity, purpose, and determination by those who were oppressed. However, one of the prerequisites for getting to this point is that black Americans must have or develop a sense of self-respect and pride in who they are and what they have accomplished. And, certainly, black America has a great deal of which to be proud.

Not only can black Americans be proud of their contributions to the building of America but also for their contributions in defending America. In 1770, Crispus

Attucks, a black American, was the first American to be killed in a series of events that would lead to the American Revolution. Attucks was the leader of a group of Americans protesting the presence of British troops in the incident that would become known as the Boston Massacre. The Boston Massacre quickly became a rallying point for those who desired independence for America. Thousands of black Americans later fought in the American Revolution and in the War of 1812.

More than two hundred thousand black Americans fought in more than two hundred battles in the Civil War and more than sixty-eight thousand died of their wounds and of disease. In spite of their high casualty rate, lower pay, other forms of racial discrimination, and the fact that black Americans were executed instead of being taken as prisoners by Confederate troops, desertion among black Americans was fifty percent lower than it was for the rest of the Union army. And, in spite of continued racism and discrimination both in civilian life and in the military, tens of thousands of black Americans fought honorably and died bravely in the Spanish American War, World War I, and World War II.

The fact is that America was never a nation of only white people, built only by white people, only for white people. America was a country of red Americans built in large measure by black Americans. Would America have become the great nation that it became or would it have happened as quickly without black Americans? It certainly would not have. One reason is that black

26

Americans have contributed to the building of America over a longer period of time than any other ethnic group.

Native Americans are the only living people indigenous to America. After Native Americans, black Americans, as a people, are the next most indigenous ethnic group in America. A decade after the first permanent English settlement was established, blacks began arriving in America. An estimated ten to fourteen million more blacks reached America before January, 1808 when the United States prohibited further importation of slaves. The slave trade did not end immediately and hundreds of thousands more Africans were illegally brought to America prior to the Civil War. Even so, from 1808 to the present, a period of almost two hundred years, less than three million blacks were illegally brought to or legally immigrated to America.

The so-called American "melting pot" occurred for blacks Americans more than a century before it occurred for most white Americans. Most of the race mixing between blacks and whites of European descent took place prior to the Civil War and most of these white Americans could trace their ancestry to pre-Revolution days. The other contribution to the black American racial mixture came from Native Americans. For these reasons, even at the end of the twentieth century, the ancestry of more than ninety percent of all black Americans, on both sides of their family, dates back to 1808 or earlier. It would be remarkable if more than one percent of white Americans can make this same claim.

As the number of blacks arriving in America slowed to a trickle, the great waves of white immigrants coming to America was just beginning. From 1815 to 1914, approximately thirty-five million white immigrants arrived in America, with twenty-five of the thirty-five million arriving after the Civil War. And it is important to note that in 1860, just before the start of the Civil War, the total population of the country was just over thirty million.

As a people, African-American roots are deeper in the United States than the roots of Anglo-Americans, Italian-Americans, Irish-Americans, Polish-Americans, German-Americans, Russian-Americans, Mexican-Americans, Chinese-Americans and every other ethnic group except Native Americans. The fact that most white Americans are able to easily identify their ethnic heritage clearly speaks to this point. It is not because they have researched their ethnic origins. It is because they have first hand knowledge of grandparents or great-grandparents who immigrated to America.

Indeed, more than one hundred million white Americans, more than forty percent of their total population, have ancestors that were processed through the Ellis Island immigration center. Ellis Island was the largest but only one of many immigration centers and it only operated from the 1890's until 1954. The facts are that black Americans, as a people, have been in America from the beginning and almost everyone else has just gotten off the boat.

White Americans created "Black America" more than three and a half centuries ago. They did so in order to isolate and exclude black Americans from their fair share of the country they were helping to build. While white America's strategy has worked for much of black America's painful but proud history, it is this same isolation and exclusion that has always provided black America with the unity, the purpose, and the determination to persevere. Black America must now maintain this union of spirit, resolve, and history for as long as it takes for black Americans to become full and equal participants in the America they worked so long and so hard to create.

In The Foreseeable Future, There Will Be Racism In America

Race is an issue in America today. Race has been an issue for almost four centuries and it will be an issue in the twenty-first century and beyond. The race issue is so deeply rooted and is such an inexorable part of American culture because, on many levels, America was built on a foundation of racism.

Racism is "the belief that race is the primary determinant of human traits and capacities and racial differences produce an inherent superiority of a particular race." Racism argues against the "self-evident" truth that "all men are created equal" and racism was perfectly acceptable in America in 1776. Racism is the explanation for one hundred and fifty-seven years of Slavery prior to 1776 and eighty-nine years of Slavery after 1776. Regardless of any and all other factors, Slavery could not have existed without boundless racism as a basis. Were it not for racism, the most important race issue in America today might well be the date or the route of the Crispus Attucks' Day Parade.

This is not to say that all the founding fathers or that the vast majority of Americans who lived in 1776 were innate, unyielding, soulless racists. It is to say that there was more than enough racism for Slavery to be permitted in the new republic. Even those who clearly saw the evils of Slavery had their own reasons and rationales to compromise their principles. First and foremost, there was the need or desire to form a nation. If Slavery had not been permitted within the new Union, it still would have existed in those colonies that would have responded by not becoming a part of the Union.

Other justifications for the continuation of Slavery included economic considerations and the logistical problem of what to do with the nearly one million black Americans who comprised almost one-fifth of the total population of the colonies. Beyond these factors, there was the consideration that most white Americans were not directly involved in Slavery and were busy pursuing their own agendas. Besides, by 1776, Slavery had been an integral part of America for more than a century and a half. If Slavery was a problem, what did it matter if the problem was resolved now or resolved at some point in the future?

While all of this may explain a lot, it still does not explain how America came to be, and continues to be, one of the most racist countries in the world. After all, unlike much older European nations, America was founded as a Christian country with ideology proclaiming that all men are created equal and with liberty and justice for all. America was the country where people came to escape the inequities and the oppression of an autocratic world. America was a country without class and caste barriers. It was a country where success was determined by hard work and talent and not merely by the circumstances of one's birth.

The American Revolution was fought to break away from the injustice and tyranny of Great Britain. And yet, in what can only be viewed as a case of paradoxical irony, in 1833, Great Britain peacefully outlawed slavery. On the other hand, it took America another thirty-two years to make Slavery illegal and then only after a bloody four-year civil war that almost destroyed the young nation.

The explanation for America's enduring bitter core of racism is also a case of paradoxical irony. From the very beginning of Slavery in America, there were those who were vehemently against it. It just did not sit well with many of the early Americans who had come to the so-called New World to escape class, ethnic, and religious oppression. Nor did Slavery sit well with those who truly believed in equality and justice for all and the other principles upon which the Union was formed.

In response, there was only one possible argument to be made by those who benefited or hoped to benefit from Slavery. That argument was that "race is the primary determinant of human traits and capacities and racial differences produce an inherent superiority of a particular race." Therefore, while antislavery arguments might be quite compelling, such arguments would be applicable only if slaves were white. Since slaves were black and blacks were inferior beings, for a dyed-in-the-wool racist, the antislavery arguments were all irrelevant.

There were a number of specific racist rationales and justifications used to dismiss those who would destroy the lifestyle and the economy of the South by eliminating Slavery. In the beginning, it was the contention of those who favored Slavery that the "all-wise Creator" had perfectly adapted the black man to the labor needs of the South. Whereas whites would die, blacks could thrive in the swamps and under the hot sun to raise the cotton and sugar crops that were necessary for the prosperity of the South. It was also argued that, because of the uncivilized, barbaric nature of blacks, they needed the "training" of plantation life for a generation or two in order to understand American laws and customs and to be successfully assimilated into American society.

As these and other rationales became more and more untenable, doctors, scientists, and pseudo-scientists argued that there was a physiological basis for supposed temperamental and intellectual differences between whites and blacks. Many carried racism to an even further extreme by arguing that blacks were not Homo sapiens, that they actually belonged to a completely different species than whites.

These and other racist arguments were being made by those who favored Slavery for more than one hundred and fifty years before the American Revolution, the signing of the Declaration of Independence, and the passage of the Constitution of the United States. The harder antislavery forces pushed for the abolition of Slavery, the more entrenched pro-slavery forces became in their racist justifications and rationales. In any case, by the time of the Civil War, racist arguments had been made for the continuation of Slavery for almost two and a half centuries.

The longer Slavery had continued, the more it had become interwoven into the fabric of America's agricultural and commercial life. In fact, many of those who were in favor of the continuation of Slavery believed themselves to be on a mission to save the economy of the South if not the economy of the entire nation. Fortunately, after the Civil War, America's agricultural and commercial life survived without Slavery. Unfortunately, two hundred and forty-six years of relentless and unwavering racist arguments also survived. And, for the past one hundred and twenty-five years, those who believed these racist arguments have passed them down to their children and their children's children.

For almost four hundred years, racism and issues resulting from racism have been the most consistent, contentious, and divisive issues that America has had to face. Before it was abolished, Slavery was the subject of statewide and national debates and a deciding factor in almost every presidential election. Even the westward expansion of the country always required an agreement or a compromise on whether Slavery would be permitted or not permitted in each new state or territory. And, of course, one of the most tragic and costly results of

Slavery and the racism that was used to justify it was the American Civil War. More Americans were killed in this four-year struggle than the sum total of all the Americans killed in every war before or since.

Black America has long criticized white America for what it sees as white America's failure to come to terms with racism and race issues in America. One of the most conspicuous examples of this unwillingness or inability to see the truth about racism is how the American Civil War is explained. American history books still list the causes of and reasons for the Civil War in terms of state rights, economics, North versus South lifestyles, climate, natural resources, regional differences in general, and, of course, Slavery. Many history books list and explain the reasons for the war based on some type of hierarchy and some even assign relative significance to the causes. However, none of them definitively state that Slavery was the principle cause, perhaps the only cause, but certainly the root cause of the Civil War. It is more than a reasonable proposition that if there had never been Slavery in America, there would have never been an American Civil War.

None of the other factors by themselves or in any combination would have resulted in the Civil War. Indeed, a number of factors would not have existed or been as consequential if it were not for Slavery. How could the South not have developed a "different way of life" with a population of eight million whites owning four million slaves? The differences in the economies of the North and South would not have been as pronounced if Slavery had not allowed the South to develop a system of extensive plantations to support "king cotton." And, if Slavery had never existed in America, by the time of the Civil War the most important state rights issue would not have been whether a state had the right to choose to be a slave state.

Even Abraham Lincoln was reluctant to admit that his war to save the Union was being fought as a result of Slavery. It took him until 1863 to issue his Emancipation Proclamation, which freed very few slaves, but made it clear to the nation and to the world the war was being fought to end Slavery. The Emancipation Proclamation was issued to boost moral at a time when Northerners were beginning to question why they were fighting such a prolonged and bloody war. And, even though the South was the world's leading supplier of cotton, the Emancipation Proclamation made it virtually impossible for France or Britain, having abolished slavery decades earlier, to then side with the slave owners of the South.

Many black Americans believe they know why white America will not or can not fully come to terms with racism and race issues in America. Their explanations range from guilt to it being human nature to avoid unpleasant issues whenever possible to do so. Another possibility is that white America simply can not comprehend or fully appreciate racism and race issues because they seldom directly affect white Americans.

The vast majority of white Americans can and do live their lives without having to, on a day to day basis, deal with or even think about racism or race issues. Black Americans do not have this option. They are a part of a racial minority and they must deal with this reality each and every day of their lives. Black Americans may have historically been known as Colored, Negroes, or African-Americans, but they will always be, first and foremost, "black Americans."

Fortunately for today's black Americans, they rarely have to deal with overt racism. During the Slavery era, racism was the norm. A minimum of ninety-five percent of what black Americans could or could not do in America was dictated solely by their race. During the Jim Crow era, black Americans lived in a distinctly racist society but they did get their first taste of freedom and opportunity. Depending on various factors, between forty and sixty percent of what black Americans could or could not do in America was based on their race. During the Equal Opportunity era, black Americans have their first real chance for success in America based on their knowledge and skills. Today, less than ten percent of what black Americans can or can not do in America is dictated by race.

It would be foolish or disingenuous for anyone to argue that racism no longer exists in America. Most back Americans would argue that somewhere between twenty-five and seventy-five percent of all white Americans, on some level, harbor racist beliefs about black Americans.

And because racism is a belief that is fueled by ignorance and hate, as long as there is ignorance and hate in America, there will be racism.

Black Americans can live with racism. They always have and, undoubtedly, they always will. They can detest racists and deplore racism but they need be genuinely concerned only when racists or racism threatens their civil rights. In the mean time, black Americans have a much more important and formidable task ahead of them. They must find ways of dealing effectively with the issues that have resulted from more than three and a half centuries of government sponsored or government tolerated racism.

The current generation of white Americans should not be proud of their racist history but it is not a requirement that they be ashamed of it. Black Americans need not be proud of their history of Slavery but they certainly have no reason to be ashamed of it. After all, it is history and the current generation of black Americans and white Americans had no part in creating it. It is something that black Americans and white Americans inherited.

What should be important to the current generation of black Americans and white Americans is how we are conducting our personal lives and where we are leading our nation. After all, we are in the process of making the history and creating the legacies that our descendents will one day inherit.

Black America Must Take A Look At The People In The Mirror

White Americans do not understand black Americans. They can be forgiven because most black Americans do not understand black Americans. Most black Americans do not understand what caused black Americans to become the people they are today. Therefore, most black Americans can not explain who or what black Americans are today. Most black Americans do not understand the basic nature of black Americans, what makes them unique, what makes them special, or what makes them "black." Most black Americans can not explain what makes black beautiful.

Most black Americans do not have enough knowledge of history to appreciate the general lessons that are to be learned from history. Even worse, they do not have enough knowledge of their own history to understand where they come from and what they have become. Of course, the same is true for most white Americans. The general consensus is that history is dry and boring and the least number of history classes that are required, the better. For white Americans, this is an unfortunate attitude. For black Americans, it is a detrimental attitude. The difference is that white America's history is presented as glory-filled, positive affirmations of the many successes of white Americans. Unfortunately, black Americans must rummage through whitewashed white history and whitewashed or half-told black history in order to find the glory-filled, positive affirmations of the many successes of black Americans.

When black Americans are taught American history, it is the history of white America. Even when black Americans are taught world history, it is the history of the white world. Early in their academic careers, most black Americans learn about World War II and the Holocaust. The word "holocaust" is an Old Testament sacrificial term that is defined as "thorough destruction, especially by fire." Almost all dictionaries also list "Holocaust" as a proper noun to define the persecution and genocidal slaughter of European Jews by Nazi Germany before and during World War II.

Over a period of twelve years, European Jews were attacked, tormented, and murdered. Their property was confiscated or destroyed. Jewish families were torn apart, frightened children were snatched from the arms of their grieving parents, and many Jewish women were the victims of rape. Some Jews were subjected to unethical medical experiments, other were used as slave laborers, and still others had to endure the horrors of concentration camps for many weeks or months. Ultimately, more than six million Jews died as a result of starvation, by firing squads and electrocution, and in gas chambers that at times operated twenty-four hours a day.

One can not help being dismayed and disheartened by this episode of man's inhumanity to his fellow man. However, one should not conclude that the wanton and abject cruelty heaped upon the Jewish people by Nazi Germany was humankind's only or most grievous case of man's inhumanity to man. Unfortunately, there have been a number of "holocaust type" episodes in the history of humankind.

There are stories of the destruction of nations in the Old Testament of the Bible as well as historical evidence of a number of mass executions in ancient times. These holocaust type episodes continued with the persecution of early Christians at the hands of the Romans and, as recently as the 1970's, more than one million Cambodians were put to death by Pol Pot and his followers, the Khmer Rouge. With estimates of up to fifty million deaths, World War II itself certainly qualifies as a holocaust type episode in the history of humankind. And, of course, there is "Slavery."

Slavery more than qualifies as a holocaust type episode in the annals of human history. In fact, black America should insist that, in addition to the current definitions of "slavery," it should also be defined as a proper noun with the definition being "the institution of slavery in the United States during the 246 year period from 1619 to 1865." After all, there is no more definitive instance of the institution of slavery in the history of humankind. If it is appropriate for history to record what happened to Jews as the "Holocaust," it is certainly appropriate for history to record what happened to Africans and black Americans as "Slavery."

The Voyage

Most Jews were ordered to report to depots where they were sent by train to be murdered or to face other horrible fates that awaited them. They were packed like cattle in locked railway cars with virtually no fresh air to breathe, very little room to move, and no toilet facilities. The small amounts of food that were available were often the result of the generosity of those who had come to the station to see their families and friends off. The many hours that Jews spent on their journey to death and destruction were degrading and filled with apprehension and fear.

The first hazard that millions of Africans had to face was being captured without getting killed or being seriously injured in the process. The next hazard was the perilous and often fatal trek of many miles from the interior of Africa to the coast. It is impossible to know how many Africans died, were maimed, or severely injured in Africa for every one slave that made it to America.

The next challenge that millions of Africans had to face was getting to America alive during the notorious Middle Passage. This was the voyage of European ships from Africa carrying slaves to be sold or traded for merchandise before the ships returned to Europe. After being chained in the airless bowels of these slave ships before they set sail, the Africans had to endure this nightmarish horror for the duration of the voyage to America. Although there are no official numbers, estimates of the mortality rate are as high as twenty percent for the inhumane, terror-filled two to three month long journey. As many as four million Africans died or were thrown overboard if they became ill or if there simply were not enough provisions to complete the journey to the Americas.

The Fate That Awaited Them

The fate of the millions of Africans who survived the horrific trip to America was not the same fate that awaited the Jews. Unlike the Jews, death did not come to these Africans in a matter of hours, days, or months. Death came only after a lifetime of psychological terror, cruel indignities, and unrelenting humiliation. Death came only after a lifetime of physical abuse, a lifetime of beatings and mutilations, and a lifetime of being raped. Death came to these Africans only after a lifetime of debasing servitude to make America the great nation it would become.

The Duration Of The Tragedy

The Holocaust began and ended in a little more than a decade. Slavery endured and thrived for two and a half centuries, almost twenty-five times longer. Whereas one generation of Jews was destroyed, more than a dozen generations of black Americans were used and discarded.

Today, Jewish children are taught of the atrocities inflicted upon their grandparents in order to give meaning to their rallying cry of "never again." On the other hand, the grandchildren of the first black slaves were already destined to the same life of debasing servitude that their parents and grandparents had lived. So too were their children, their grandchildren, and their great-grandchildren. And, even so, this would mark only the halfway point in the history of Slavery in America. Another six generations of black Americans would have to suffer the horrors of Slavery before it would finally be abolished in America.

The End Of The Tragedy

The Jewish Holocaust ended with World War II in 1945. And although the world community, through apathy and lack of resolve, had done little to prevent the Holocaust, there was no shortage of outrage when it was over. There was also a great deal of sympathy for the plight of the Jews who survived. Many people and most nations were willing to assist them in recovering from their tragedy. A number of Nazi leaders died in the war, committed suicide, or were ultimately put on trial and punished. At Nuremberg, leaders responsible for the Nazi regime of terror were convicted of various crimes, including crimes against humanity.

Although slavery was constitutionally abolished in America in 1865, it was abolished only as chattel slavery is classically defined. A form of slavery continued for many black Americans for most of the next one hundred years. When Slavery ended in 1865, the overwhelming majority of black Americans had no assets, no skills, and absolutely no education. Making this disastrous situation even worse, these black Americans lived in a world dominated by racism, a world that would deny them almost every opportunity to improve their lives.

Most black Americans living in the South had little choice but to participate in schemes such as tenant farming, also known as sharecropping. Sharecroppers reaped little or no profits from their labor and, more often than not, they were in perpetual debt to white landowners. Poll taxes, literacy tests, intimidation, and a number of other tactics were used to prevent black Americans from voting. At best, mostly in Northern cities, black Americans were occasionally given equal access, equal rights, and equal protection under the law. It was only in the late 1960's that the holocaust type episode of Slavery and the Jim Crow era finally ended for black Americans, three and a half centuries after it began.

The Aftermath

After World War II, the State of Israel was created as a Jewish homeland. It became a legitimate nation when the United States officially recognized it in 1948. As a result of its alliance with and support from the United States, today, Israel is one of the world's most highly developed and most technologically advanced nations in the world. And, despite its small size, Israel is one of the most militarily powerful nations on earth. It is generally believed that Israel has the nuclear capability to easily destroy any or all its enemies within a matter of minutes.

In the aftermath of the Holocaust, the world Jewish community united and in one voice declared they would "never again" be helpless victims of the anti-Semitism that had plagued their history. Then, with extraordinary determination and persistence, the Jewish people began doing the things required to back up their words. As part of this process, they do not depend on others to teach their children the critical lessons their children must learn. They teach their children about their long and proud history but they also teach their children about the horrors of the Holocaust. And, of course, they teach their children what they must do to ensure that such a catastrophe never happens again.

In the aftermath of three and half centuries of Slavery and oppression, history is still waiting on an appropriate response from black America. The invention of rap music does not compare to having one's own country and a nuclear arsenal.

Accepting The Realities Of Slavery

There are, of course, inherent problems in comparing historical events, and even more so when they occurred a number of years apart, in different parts of the world, for altogether different reasons. The Jewish Holocaust was a clear case of attempted genocide. Commercial slavery was all about economic exploitation. In a changing world, Slavery lasted about as long as it could have possibly lasted. If Hitler had not been stopped, one can only guess how many more millions might have died. In any case, any discussion of Slavery and the Holocaust is in no way intended to minimize the heinous atrocities and the incredible horrors of either Slavery or the Holocaust.

If the point of a discussion about Slavery and the Holocaust is not about which people suffered more or which people suffered longer, what then is the point? It is simply this. Black Americans were, and to a large extent continue to be, the victims of perhaps the most monumental holocaust in the history of humankind - and they do not even realize it. Compounding this terrible reality is the fact that black Americans do not understand why it is critical for them to recognize and deal with the holocaust called Slavery. Clearly, if black Americans do not know and understand their history, they can not possible understand who and what they are today.

To begin to understand Slavery, Black Americans must first understand that the horrors of Slavery do not justify an automatic indictment of white Americans as cruel, cold-blooded monsters who would exploit their fellow human beings for the sake of economic gain. To do so would also condemn the many black Africans who were involved in the slave trade as well as hundreds of black Americans who owned slaves other than their own family members. It would also require ignoring most of the recorded history of humankind.

For thousands of years, slavery occurred almost universally among people of every level of material culture, including ancient Egyptians, Sumerians, Greeks, Indians, Babylonians, Persians, and Romans. Slavery was so much a part of acceptable human behavior that there is nothing in the Bible or the Koran that condemns or specifically prohibits it. The Old Testament does stipulate a period of seven years as the limit for forced servitude, although this limit was rarely adhered to.

History records that slavery, indentured servitude, and other forms of human bondage once existed in virtually every country in the world and, on small scales, they still exist in many parts of the world today. It has only been within the last century or two that a majority of the world's population has lived in societies that were not based on class or caste – both being determined solely by circumstances of birth.

At one time, most land, and the people who were allowed to live on it, belonged to a pharaoh, an emperor, a czar, a king, a queen, his or her family members, or to those who were in favor with them. It was not a simple matter of working hard, saving money, and buying a small family farm. Land was passed down from generation to generation or reverted back to the head of state. America was instrumental in changing this world of class and privilege. In America there was actually good land that could be owned by common men. This is indeed what made America the land of opportunity.

We must recognize that how we view history is colored by our present-day sensibilities and our contemporary values. In many respects, our world is one hundred and eighty degrees different than it was five hundred or even only fifty years ago. Slavery existed in America at the same time that slavery existed in the rest of the world. Slavery ended in America about the same time that slavery ended in the rest of the world. Indeed, one could argue that slavery and the end of slavery were merely evolutionary steps in the continuing ascent of humankind. What then is the importance of black Americans knowing the truth about and understanding the realities of Slavery?

"We need history, not to tell us what happened or to explain the past, but to make the past alive so that it can explain us and make a future possible." (Allan Bloom, the "Cloning Of The American Mind," 1987)

The People In The Mirror

How does black America's history "explain" black Americans of today? To begin with, we must understand that two hundred and forty-six years, sixty-five percent, of black America's history consists of the Slavery era. One hundred and three years, twenty-seven percent, consists of the Jim Crow era. Thirty years, a little less than eight percent, consists of the Equal Opportunity era.

Based on these percentages, if black America's history were personified as an individual twenty-three year old black man, it would be comparable to him having spent the first fifteen years of his life continuously being physically, mentally, and sexually abused. For the next six years, until the age of twenty-one, he would have been unloved and unsupported as he moved in and out of foster homes and halfway houses. In his twenty-second and twenty-third years, he would be on his own. He would have very little education and few marketable skills. However, his greatest problem would be the tragic, trauma-filled life he had led. Without a great deal of understanding and meaningful counseling, his life would be difficult, if not impossible, to repair.

In total, ninety-two percent of the time that blacks have been in America they have lived in slavery or under conditions only a level above slavery. Clearly, the reality of these numbers is that slavery and oppression define black America. Black Americans must understand and acknowledge that, in 1999, slavery and oppression "explain" black Americans as a people.

There will always be black Americans who will argue that a better approach is to simply let go of the past and move forward into the new Equal Opportunity era. Undoubtedly, a similar argument was made to the many Jewish survivors of their Holocaust who refused to have the identification numbers tattooed on their arms removed. Admittedly, it may be easier to forget or less painful to learn to ignore trauma suffered in the past. But can black Americans afford to take this approach? Is it possible for black Americans to get to where they need to be if they do not even know where they have been?

There will also be black Americans who will be uncomfortable, if not offended, by the notion that black America needs to be "examined and explained." Their point of view might be justified if the only intent was to look for negatives about black Americans or the only expectation was to find things that are wrong with black America. There are, in fact, many more positive aspects than negative aspects about black America and black Americans. The most obvious and most dramatic is that black America has survived as a people through such a long and precarious history. In any case, any self-assessment is pointless if it is not thorough or brutally honest. And any self-assessment of black America is certainly of little or no value if it is not expressly for the purpose of making a better future for black Americans.

Finally, it should be obvious that any explanation of black America should be by black Americans, for black Americans. Black America has no reason and certainly no obligation to explain itself to white America. Besides, given the fact that racism and oppression defines and explains much of the history of white America, white Americans clearly have their own corresponding issues that they should be busy examining. In any case, at this point in black America's history, it is not important what white America thinks of black America. It is only important what black America thinks of itself.

How do black Americans "make the past alive so that it can explain us and make a future possible"? The first step is for black Americans to make an investment in the time and effort required to learn the history of black America. Secondly, based on their history, black Americans must take a look in the mirror and make a straightforward, brutally honest assessment of who and what they are. Only then will black Americans begin to understand the critical issues to explore and the important questions to ask.

- Is it possible to inflict damage on the psyche of a people as a result of more than three and a half centuries of slavery and oppression?
- Are there psychological ramifications that black Americans must deal with as a result of sixteen consecutive generations being told that they are "animals" and that their only value is in doing physical labor?
- Did three hundred and forty-nine years of black Americans being told that they are "helpless children" and "the white man's burden" create a welfare mentality in black America?
- Are there physiological consequences for black Americans as a result of two and a half centuries of "slave breeding," "slave food," backbreaking labor, and habitual physical abuse?

These are only a few of the questions that should be asked as part of the dozens of issues that need to be explored. Of course, all of the answers will be opened to debate and, more times than not, consensus will be unlikely. Fortunately, consensus is not the objective. Black Americans getting a better perspective of who they are by virtue of knowing where they come from is the important part of the process. And it is only as a result of the entire process of honest assessment and informed acceptance that black America will be able to move forward with pride, dignity, and confidence.

Black Americans need only remember that the true measure of a people is not only how far they have gone, nor only how far they have come. The true measure of a people is also how much farther they have the vision to go.

The Struggle For Civil Rights In America Is Over

The struggle is over. The war that was fought to obtain and guarantee civil rights for black Americans ended three decades ago. Contrary to what many black Americans believe, black America won the war.

The meaning of "civil rights" has changed over the years. When the Bill of Rights, the first ten amendments to the Constitution, was enacted, the intent was to place limits on the government in favor of individual liberty. Since that time, the scope of civil rights has evolved to also include protection from arbitrary or discriminatory treatment by groups or individuals. Although all black Americans should know the complete history of the Civil Rights movement, black Americans, especially black children, should know the basic facts about this struggle.

In 1954, in *BROWN V. BOARD OF EDUCATION OF TOPEKA, KANSAS*, the United States Supreme Court declared that segregation in public schools was unconstitutional. The court acknowledged what black Americans had always known: separate educational facilities were "inherently unequal." This decision effectively reversed the 1896 *PLESSY V. FURGUSON* Supreme Court decision that upheld the principle of "separate but equal" facilities for blacks and whites. It was this decision that had led to the profusion of Jim Crow laws and instituted the system of legal segregation in America.

In 1957 and 1960, the United States Congress passed laws to protect the rights of black voters. However, in the 1964 elections, it was demonstrated that these laws were not effective. Immediately after Dr. Martin Luther King, Jr. led a march from Selma to Montgomery, Alabama to dramatize the problem, the Voting Rights Act of 1965 was passed. The Voting Rights Act went so far as to authorize the attorney general of the United States, under some circumstances, to send federal examiners to register black Americans to vote.

The Civil Rights Act of 1964 was also the result of the pressure of the Civil Rights movement. This legislation prohibited discrimination in employment, established the Equal Employment Opportunity Commission, and banned discrimination in public accommodations. The Civil Rights Act of 1968 was the final major piece of civil rights legislation to be passed by Congress. It prohibited discrimination in housing and real estate.

There were many victories, large and small, in black America's successful struggle for civil rights. Many of the most significant of these victories were won during the lifetime of the current generation of black Americans or their parents. It is unfortunate that so few black Americans are aware of these events or appreciate their historical significance. It is unfortunate that black

Americans do not insist that their children learn about these events that have such a profound affect on their lives.

Without a sense of history, black Americans can not fully comprehend the inhumane, disheartening, and changeless nature of Slavery. Without a sense of history, black Americans can not deplore the inequity and the injustice of the Jim Crow era. Without a sense of history, black Americans can not appreciate the opportunity to succeed in America that was made possible by the success of the Civil Rights movement.

An amazing array of heroes contributed to black America's successful struggle to obtain civil rights: Frederick Douglass, Booker T. Washington, W.E.B. DuBois, George Washington Carver, Jesse Owens, Daniel Hale Williams, A. Philip Randolph, Jackie Robinson, Ralph Bunche, Thurgood Marshall, Rosa Parks, Medgar and James Evers, Martin Luther King, Jr., and Malcolm X. These are but a few of the heroes of the struggle. All black Americans should know their names and the contributions they made.

Beyond the well-known, popular heroes, black America's struggle for civil rights was a victory by the people. Many thousands sacrificed their lives for the cause. Hundreds of thousands contributed their time and money. Millions contributed their hopes, their dreams, and their prayers. All black Americans stood as one and demanded equality and justice. In the end, after three and a half centuries of oppression, black Americans won the same equal access, equal rights, and equal protection under the law that white Americans had enjoyed since 1776.

If one is looking for evidence that black America has won its struggle for civil rights, it can be found by simply talking to their parents or grandparents who were alive during the Jim Crow era. They will attest to a time not so long ago when they attended segregated schools, when they could not play professional sports in all-white leagues, and when they were forced to serve their country in all-black military units. They will attest to a time not so long ago when they had to drink from separate water fountains, use separate restroom facilities, and enter through the back doors of white establishments. They will attest to a time not so long ago when they had to ride in the back of the bus, when they could not vote, and when they knew of at least one black American who had been lynched.

Certainly, by these measurements, in 1999, the civil rights of most black Americans are seldom, if ever, violated. Additionally, when the civil rights of black Americans are now violated, they have legal recourse that can and should be used to remedy the injustice. Admittedly, the civil rights of some black and white Americans are violated every day in every state of the Union. On the other hand, every day, millions of white Americans are very careful not to do anything that might give the impression they are violating the civil rights of black Americans.

Black America's struggle for civil rights is over. All that remains is for black Americans to be aware of these rights, to be vigilant in the protection of these rights, and if necessary, be prepared to fight and even die to preserve these rights. It was this level of dedication that resulted in victory and only this level of dedication will secure this victory for all time.

Black America Has Won Its Struggle For Civil Rights In America

Many black Americans simply do not believe the struggle for civil rights in America is over. And almost all black Americans, on some level, are reluctant to accept the fact that black America actually won the war. In some cases, the reasons for the doubts are based on history. In most cases, the skepticism is the result of misconceptions about the nature and the objectives of the civil rights struggle.

Considering the history of the struggle, it is not very difficult to understand why black America is reluctant to declare victory. After all, this is not the first time black Americans have had sound, logical reasons to believe they had won the war. Three years after Slavery was abolished, civil rights for black Americans was proclaimed in and guaranteed by the United States Constitution, the sacred document that is the very foundation of our democracy.

The 14th Amendment, ratified in 1868, states that "All persons born or naturalized in the United States, and subject to the jurisdiction thereof, are citizens of the United States and of the State wherein they reside. No State shall make or enforce any law which shall abridge the privileges or immunities of citizens of the United States; nor shall any State deprive any person of life, liberty, or property, without due process of law; nor deny to any person within its jurisdiction the equal protection of the laws." The 15th Amendment, ratified in 1870, states that "The right of citizens of the United States to vote shall not be denied or abridged by the United States or by any State on account of race, color, or previous condition of servitude."

Could the words or their intent be any clearer? In fact, for more than one hundred years, the 14th and 15th Amendments to the Constitution were used as arguments against additional civil rights legislation. Those who opposed such legislation contended that it was unnecessary given that the 14th and 15th Amendments made black Americans citizens of the United States and guaranteed them the same civil rights enjoyed by white citizens.

Yet, even before the official ratification of the 13th Amendment that ended Slavery, "Black Codes" were being used in the South in an attempt to restore a form of quasi-slavery. It was this blatant disregard of the 13th Amendment, clearly denying black Americans their civil rights, which led to the passage of the 14th and 15th Amendments to the Constitution. It was this same determination to deny black Americans their civil rights that led to the passage of the Civil Rights Acts of 1866, 1870, 1871, and 1875.

So, then, why should black Americans believe that they have indeed won the war at this point in their history? What are the differences between the "first civil rights victory" of the latter part of the nineteenth century and the "latest civil rights victory" of the latter part of the twentieth century?

One obvious difference is that the latest civil rights victory has lasted longer. It has, in fact, lasted more than thirty years. On the other hand, the first civil rights victory lasted barely a decade and it lasted that long only because of military force in the form of federal troops. The Compromise of 1877 allowed the election of Rutherford B. Hayes to the presidency. However, the price to be paid was the promise that federal troops would be removed from the South. This compromise ended the Reconstruction era and effectively reversed black America's first civil rights victory.

In addition to the longevity of black America's second civil rights victory, there is another reason why black Americans can believe their latest victory will not be snatched away from them. This reason is based on "the times" in which the two victories were achieved.

In the latter part of the nineteenth century, white America was not prepared to give black Americans equal access, equal rights, and equal protection under the law. At the same time, black America was not in a position to demand these rights. In the latter part of the twentieth century, white America understands that black America will accept nothing less. Just as black Americans would

65

have fought any attempt to return them to Slavery after they were freed, black Americans have made it clear that they are willing and able to fight any attempt to return them to the Jim Crow era now that they have obtained civil rights. It is this difference in attitude, resolve, and resources that assures black America that its latest civil rights victory will endure.

Even so, some black Americans do not believe that the struggle for civil rights is over because of misconceptions about the nature and objectives of the struggle for civil rights. The terms "civil rights" and "equal rights" are generally interchangeable; however, neither term should be mistaken for any other type of "equality."

Black America's struggle for civil rights has always been about equal access, equal rights, and equal protection under the law. It is not about social equality, economic equality, or any other type of equality. These distinctions are not trivial and, for a number of reasons, understanding these distinctions is critical for the future progress and success of black America.

By accepting that it has won its struggle for civil rights, black America will acknowledge a monumental accomplishment that was more than one hundreds years in the making. The current generation of black Americans can be proud of this accomplishment because it honors their contributions to the cause. Even more importantly, accepting that black America has won its struggle for civil rights would honor all those who came before this generation.   It would honor all of their contributions and it would honor all of their sacrifices that led to the final victory.

Beyond the honor and beyond the pride of having won a long and hard fought victory, there is an even more important reason for black Americans to delineate between their successful struggle to obtain civil rights and the next challenge they must face.

Black Americans can view their struggle for "absolute equality" in America as a war.   In a war, there are campaigns, with campaigns consisting of any number of battles.   Just as an army needs to know when a battle or a campaign has been won, black America needs to recognize when a struggle has been won.   If an army stands around after a battle is over, it risks the possibility of losing the next battle, the campaign, or even the war. This is surely true of black America's struggle to reach absolute equality in America.

Black Americans do not have time to be confused, and after almost four centuries of oppression, they do not have the luxury of standing still.   They must declare victory in the struggle for civil rights.   They must decide on their next objective.   They must prepare a battle plan for that objective and they must begin to execute it.   This is what black Americans must do in order to move forward.   This is what black Americans must do in order to reach their goal of "absolute equality" in America; equality in every sense of the word.

"Eternal Vigilance Is The Price Of Liberty"

For almost four hundred years, black Americans have proven themselves to be a courageous, resilient, resolute, and honorable people. More so than any other ethnic group in America, there is little or nothing in the history of black America for which black Americans should be ashamed. There is, however, one thing that should be a source of embarrassment and regret for all black Americans. It is the voting record of black Americans during the first thirty years of the Equal Opportunity era.

With the exception of sporadic organized efforts to elect or defeat specific candidates, black voter turnout is chronically low. America is currently a nation where just over half its citizens who are eligible even bother to register to vote. Of those who are registered, less than half may vote in any given election. It is disheartening that black America should be on the low end of these appalling statistics. It can be argued that voting ought to be a litmus test for the right to call oneself a decent, worthy, or honorable black American.

There are three major reasons why black Americans should consider voting not only a cherished right but also a sacred duty.

The first reason is exemplified by the maxim "eternal vigilance is the price of liberty." Black America has won its struggle for civil rights and black Americans can be assured there will be no wholesale abrogation of these rights. Given the current laws and a track record of conscientious and equitable enforcement of these laws, there would seem to be little danger of black America being forced back into the Jim Crow era from which it emerged three decades ago. Yet, nothing in life is guaranteed. During the 20th century, at least ten million people have been killed simply because they did not share the same race, religion, or ethnicity of those who were in power.

Voting is the single best way for all Americans, and especially black Americans, to protect their rights. In an autocracy, it is the gun and the bullet, the force of arms, which sustains unlimited government power. In a representative democracy, it is the vote that legitimizes and directs those who govern, thereby limiting the power of government. Clearly, it is the power, or the lack of power, of the vote that defines various forms of government. Voting is the "vigilance," the price that all Americans must pay at every possible opportunity to maintain our system of government. This is especially true for black Americans. Voting is the best way, if not the only way, to ensure that the victories won by black America will endure.

The second reason why voting should be a sacred duty for all black Americans is that, in spite of what many black Americans have been brainwashed into believing, every single vote cast by a black American is a very important and extremely valuable vote.

It is important to note that "voting" is not the same as "getting involved in the political process" or even "being an informed voter." Voting is going to the polls on Election Day, marking a ballot, and placing it in the ballot box. In a perfect world, more black Americans would be involved in the political process, more black Americans would study the issues and the candidates, and more black Americans would make informed, prudent choices when they vote. However, in the imperfect world in which we live, if black Americans do none of these things, they should still vote.

If none of the candidates are worthy of being elected, black Americans should choose the lesser of the evils. If black Americans choose to vote democratic because they always have, they should just vote. If they choose to vote republican because they usually vote democratic, they should just vote. If black Americans choose to vote for third party or fourth party candidates or even write in their own names, they should just vote. When it comes to voting, black Americans should just do it.

To some, this may seem to be an unusual or extreme position. It is not. It is simply an effective use of the American democratic process. And, in a sense, it is exactly what one might expect in a capitalistic system. That is, if it were discovered that twenty-five year old ex-Marines had a billion dollars more of disposal income than previously known, American businesses would immediately come up with products and services to sell to twenty-five year old ex-Marines. Similarly, if one million additional black Americans suddenly began to vote in every possible election, politicians would quickly come up with "products and services" directed toward black Americans.

This is also the reason why there is no such thing as a wrong vote and the only wasted vote is a vote that is not cast. To a politician, a vote not cast is a "push," it benefits neither the politician nor the politician's opponent. Politicians, therefore, can not afford to waste their time and their energy on non-voters. Clearly, it is in their best interest to concentrate their efforts on voters because voters are twice as important as non-voters are. Not only can a voter penalize a candidate by not giving the candidate his or her vote - the voter also penalizes the candidate by giving his or her vote to the candidate's opponent.

Even with black Americans comprising less than fifteen percent of the total population of the United States, there would be an immediate response from politicians if sixty percent of all eligible black Americans suddenly started voting. If seventy or eighty percent started voting in every election, politicians would be lining up in black communities to ask what they can do to earn the black vote.

The third reason why voting should be considered a sacred duty for black Americans is because of the long and agonizing struggle that was required to secure their right to vote.

Thousands of dedicated and determined black and white Americans made incredible sacrifices in order to win and secure this fundamental right of democracy for black America. Hundreds of brave men, women, and children died in the struggle. A cloud of shame will hang over black America as long as it allows the sacrifices that were made and especially the lives that were lost to have all been in vain. If there is a day that a black American has a reason to be embarrassed or ashamed, it is the last Election Day that he or she did not vote.

Black Americans can accomplish three very important goals by simply voting in every election. They can preserve the rights that black America has already obtained. They can ensure that black America gets its fair share of any new benefits that are made available to the American public. And, finally, they can show their appreciation and respect to those who fought and died so that they could freely exercise their right to vote. The maximum amount of time it takes to vote is no more than one or two hours once or twice a year. The minimum amount of effort it takes to vote is to go to the polls on Election Day, mark a ballot, and place it in the ballot box.

It bears repeating. If there is a day that a black American has a reason to be embarrassed or ashamed, it is the last Election Day that he or she did not vote.

Socioeconomic Equality: A Call To Arms

Black America's struggle for "civil rights" should not be confused with black America's struggle to attain "social and economic equality" in America.

Civil rights laws guarantee citizens of the United States "equal access, equal rights, and equal protection under the law." Civil rights laws guarantee that a black American can patronize a restaurant in a predominantly white neighborhood in New York or any other city in America. These laws make it illegal for the restaurant to refuse to serve the customer because he or she is black. Civil rights laws guarantee that a black American can go to a corporate employment office in Georgia and apply for a job as a vice president of the company. These laws also make it illegal for the company to deny the applicant the job because he or she is black.

Social equality and economic equality are altogether different than civil rights. Social equality means that negative conditions such as lack of employment, crime, substance abuse, lack of education, domestic violence, divorce, and so forth are no more or less likely to impact the life of the black customer at the restaurant than any other customer in the restaurant. Economic equality means that the owner of the restaurant in the predominantly white neighborhood is just as likely to be a black American as a white American. It also means that the CEO of the company hiring the vice president is just as likely to be a black American as a white American.

The term "socioeconomic" can be defined as "relating to or involving a combination of social and economic factors." It is appropriate to consider social and economic factors in combination because in America, more so than most countries, they almost always go hand in hand. Well-paid company executives are rarely mugged as they leave their homes in exclusive neighborhoods. Owners of thriving businesses do not get arrested for selling crack cocaine on street corners. Children who are raised in two parent homes are more likely to go to college than children raised in single parent homes. More than ninety percent of the people in America's prison and jails are uneducated and were raised in families with incomes that were near or below the poverty level.

Because socioeconomic equality is an altogether different commodity than civil rights, the nature of a struggle to attain socioeconomic equality is inherently different than a struggle for civil rights. The enemy in black America's struggle for civil rights was racist and apathetic white America. This enemy was well-known, easily identified, with motives and tactics that were clearly understood by black America. Therefore, the major strategy in the struggle for civil rights was relatively straightforward. It was to focus the attention of the American public and the world community on the plight of black America and to keep the need for change in the foreground until white America relented.

Unfortunately, black Americans can not march, boycott, sit-in, or protest their way to socioeconomic equality. This is because the principal enemy in this struggle is not racist and apathetic white America. The predominate and most formidable enemies in black America's struggle for social and economic equality are black America's own lack of unity, its lack of a strategy, and its lack of education and knowledge.

The Need For A New Coalition

Unlike the struggle for civil rights, the struggle for socioeconomic equality will be an internal struggle. Most of the battles will be waged in black communities by forces of dedicated, forwarding thinking black Americans against forces of ignorance and despair. In most respects, it will be akin to a civil war.

In the struggle for civil rights, all black Americans were on the same side. "What do we want?" black ministers and black pimps shouted in unison. "Freedom" drug dealers and drug counselors yelled in reply. "When do we want it?" shouted college professors and high school dropouts. "Now" was the refrain of business owners and welfare recipients, police officers and convicts, the rich and the powerful and the poor and the powerless, and every other black man, woman, and child in America.

No one individual, program, or institution can elevate the socioeconomic status of black America. Unity is as much of a requirement in this struggle as it was in black America's struggle for civil rights. Unfortunately, in the struggle for socioeconomic equality, all black Americans will not be on the same side. In this struggle, all decent, hardworking, caring black Americans must unite against those individuals, both black and white, who have a vested interest in seeing black America fail. Unrepentant drug dealers, pimps, and gang-bangers who are not for the struggle must therefore be against it. For this reason, black America's struggle for socioeconomic equality will be no less difficult and no less dangerous than black America's struggle for civil rights.

The Requirements Of A Strategy

If black America is to be successful in its struggle for socioeconomic equality it must first develop and implement an appropriate strategy. It is not enough to say that "black America can do better." It is not enough to say that "black America will do better." What must be said is "if black America follows this specific plan, then black America will obtain these specific results."

The strategy must be as straightforward as the strategy used in the Civil Rights movement. All black Americans should be able to articulate the strategy using just a few sentences or phrases. The strategy must simultaneously address both the economic and social problems that now cripple black America. And, finally, the strategy must be inclusive. All black Americans must clearly see how they can and should contribute to the cause.

The Need For Education and Knowledge

At this point in black America's history, the major obstacle to socioeconomic equality is not the lack of civil rights. The major obstacle is that black Americans lack the education and knowledge to successfully compete with the rest of America. If tens of thousands more black Americans were educated and trained professionals, there would be tens of thousands more gainfully employed black Americans. Unless and until black America reaches educational equality with white America, it will never reach socioeconomic equality with white America.

Clearly, the lack of knowledge and education within black America today is the result of Slavery and institutionalized racism of the past. For three and a half centuries, keeping black Americans uneducated and ignorant was white America's strategy for maintaining its socioeconomic standing. Clearly, black America's strategy for attaining socioeconomic equality must now be built around the education and the enlightenment of black Americans.

The struggle for civil rights and the struggle for socioeconomic equality should not be confused. The most important relationship between the two is that obtaining civil rights is a prerequisite for socioeconomic equality. That is, it is virtually impossible for a minority to successfully attain social and economic equality without having first obtained civil rights. This would certainly explain the failure of black America to make significant economic gains during the Jim Crow era. However, now that black America is in the Equal Opportunity era, for the first time since their arrival in America, black Americans have a fair and equal opportunity to pursue the great American dream.

Black Americans Will Never Get "Forty Acres And A Mule"

During the first thirty years of the Equal Opportunity era, black America has made very little progress in its struggle for social and economic equality. Black America had the lowest socioeconomic standing in America in the 1960's and black America still has the lowest socioeconomic standing in America three decades later.

It would, in fact, be more encouraging if it could be reported that black America's lack of progress was the result of a faulty plan or a failed strategy. Unfortunately, this is not the case. There is no evidence that black America made an honest, realistic assessment of its relative strengths and weaknesses. There is no evidence that black America examined and evaluated its assets and liabilities. There is no evidence that black America determined what was necessary to reach socioeconomic equality. And there is no evidence that black America then initiated a plan to reach socioeconomic equality.

Looking back over the past thirty years, one could easily conclude that black America's expectation was to slowly reach socioeconomic equality, one black American at a time, over a period of many decades. If there was a strategy associated with this goal of "eventually reaching socioeconomic equality," it was to depend on white America to rescue black America by providing black Americans with some type or manner of "reparations."

The concept of reparations is as old as the maxim "to the victors go the spoils." In the past, the winning side simply looted the losing country and often even enslaved the losing people. In recent, more civilized times, the winning side often determines a dollar amount or other compensation that it declares the loser must pay. The intent of such reparations is to reimburse the winning side for the financial burden of fighting the war as well as to compensate those on the winning side for their pain and suffering.

The idea of reparations for black Americans began in earnest as the American Civil War ended. Before then, it was enough to simply dream of the day that all black Americans would be delivered from Slavery. In March of 1863, Congress created the Bureau of Refugees, Freedmen, and Abandoned Lands, or simply the Freedmen's Bureau. This agency was authorized to issue "provisions, clothing and fuel" for "destitute and suffering refugees and freedmen." The bureau was empowered to set aside abandoned or confiscated land within the defeated Confederacy and to assign at a fair rent "to every male citizen, whether refugee or freeman" a parcel "not more than forty acres of such land." This is the origin of the notion that black Americans were entitled to and would eventually receive reparations for Slavery. Thus began the myth of "forty acres and a mule."

It is a reasonable notion that black Americans are entitled to some form of compensation for having been forced to endure the pain and suffering of Slavery for two hundred and forty-six years. Most black Americans learned all that they know about Slavery from watching the televising of "Roots." This graphic, heart-wrenching television series did convey a sense of the length of time, from generation to generation, that black America had to endure Slavery. However, this series could not adequately depict the horrific truth about Slavery for the entire lifetime of any one black American.

"Roots" could not make black Americans understand the cruelty of being indoctrinated as a toddler into the institution of Slavery. The series could not make black Americans comprehend what it was like to toil in cotton fields under a hot Mississippi sun for as far back as one could remember. It was impossible for "Roots" to reveal to black Americans the dismal, sad, and painful life of any one individual slave. One can only try to imagine working from dawn to dusk, hour after hour, day after day, week after week, month after month, year after year until dropping dead from exhaustion and malnutrition, broken and crippled, and not yet forty years old.

Aside from the pain and suffering aspects of any claim by black America for reparations, there is also the matter of two hundred and forty-six years of uncompensated labor. While some white Americans may debate the degree to which black Americans contributed to the building of our country, there can be no doubt that America would not have become as great a nation as quickly as it became one without the contributions of black Americans. The economy of the South provides some proof of this fact. More than one hundred and thirty years have passed since the Civil War ended and, without its unlimited source of free labor, the South still has not reclaimed its ante-bellum economic glory.

It would certainly seem that black America has a legitimate claim to some form of reparation or compensation for twelve generations of forced, uncompensated labor, not to mention the pain and suffering of being enslaved. After all, America is a country where a person may be awarded millions of dollars for spilling hot coffee in his or her lap or for not being told how to correctly use a ladder or a pail.

If every black American were awarded one hundred dollars, the total would be about three billion dollars. This is considerably less than the part of our federal budget that is misappropriated or "misplaced" each year. If every black American were awarded one thousand dollars, the total would be about thirty billion dollars. This may seem to be a huge sum, but with annual federal budgets over one trillion dollars, it certainly could be done over a period of time with absolutely no negative ramifications on the American economy.

In any case, it will never happen. It is that simple. Slavery ended almost one hundred and thirty-five years ago and it has not happen yet and there are no reasonable scenarios that would lead to it happening in the next one hundred and thirty-five years. On the other hand, there are two very sound reasons why black Americans will not receive reparations from white America for Slavery or for Jim Crow era oppression. The first reason is that white America does not choose to give every black American "forty acres and a mule." The second reason is that white America is not obligated to give every black American "forty acres and a mule."

Undoubtedly, the most appropriate time for black America to have received reparations in the form of land was in the years following the Civil War. However, arguments can be made as to why this was or was not practical or even possible.

Why Reparations Were Not Possible

Even though black America was on the winning side in the Civil War, it must be remembered that it was a civil war with the resources of the North and the resources of the South pitted against each other. When the war was over, these two severely damaged halves came back together as one devastated nation, having spent at least twenty billion dollars to wage the war. Even, if the country could have afforded reparations they would have been made primarily in the South where more than ninety percent of all black Americans lived.

This uneven distribution of the black population was also a big part of the problem.

At the beginning of the Civil War, the population of the slave states was comprised of eight million white Americans and four million slaves. After the devastation of the Civil War, there was barely enough left of the Southern economy to support the two-thirds of the population that was white. However, even if the Southern economy was not in ruins, there was still the question of where free land for millions of blacks would have come from. Almost three-fourths of all white Southerners had no connection with slavery through either direct ownership or family ties. The "typical" Southerner was a small farmer who did not own slaves.

<u>Why Reparations Were Possible And Practical</u>

Even with devastation of the Southern economy and the tremendous financial cost of the Civil War to the entire country, it was possible to have given black Americans reparations in the form of free land with little or no expense to the taxpayers of America.

At the end of Civil War, there were only thirty-six states in the Union. The land that would be used to create the remaining twelve states, including almost all of the larger western states, was still largely unsettled. As late as April 22, 1889, the United States government was just opening up the Oklahoma Territory for settlement. In less than twenty-four hours, more than two million acres were staked out and claimed by white Americans, many of whom had recently immigrated to America.

Where were black Americans during this and the other large land giveaways by the United States government? They were still in the South, just beginning one hundred years of sharecropping, debt peonage, and migrant labor.

Clearly, after the Civil War, white America did not want to give black Americans reparations for two hundred and forty-six years of Slavery. Clearly, white America now has no desire to compensate black Americans for an additional one hundred and three years of Jim Crow era oppression. It took three hundred and forty-nine years for America, the land of liberty and justice for all, to even reluctantly admit that it was not treating a large segment of its population fairly. It took three and a half centuries and black Americans burning down cities before white America finally agreed to give equal access, equal rights, and equal protection under the law to its black citizens.

It has always been, at best, unrealistic for black Americans to believe that white America would assist in elevating their socioeconomic standing. After all, black Americans are the people who white Americans have historically stood upon to elevate their own socioeconomic status. From most of white America's perspective, there is only so much land, there is only so much wealth, and there is only so much power. If, therefore, black America is going to suddenly share in this land, wealth, or power, it has to come from somewhere. And the question that white Americans ask is "why should my socioeconomic status be lowered to correct a problem that I personally had no part in creating?"

After almost four centuries, black America should realize that white America's answer to this question is and will forever be that "my socioeconomic status should not be lowered to correct a problem that I personally had no part in creating." But, more importantly, black America must realize that there is nothing that it can do to force white America to share in its ill-gotten gains.

From white America's perspective, it is the judge and the jury and it has ruled that the statute of limitations has expired. It may not be fair but life is not always fair. After all, the world is still waiting on and will probably never collect the billions of dollars of reparations that were levied upon Germany and other countries after World War I and World War II.

Unfortunately for black America, white America's assessment of the situation is essentially correct. Fortunately for black Americans, they now have the opportunity to say to white America, "we are dedicated to getting the forty acres and a mule that you cheated us out of and then we are coming after some of yours."

There Will Never Be A Marshall Plan For Black America

Prior to the "Geneva Convention" of 1864, there were no international rules governing the conduct of men engaged in warfare. Prisoners were tortured and killed, the wounded went untreated, and the dead were left unburied. "To the victors go the spoils" was more than an expression. It was normal behavior for the winners of a battle or a war to simply loot, rape, and pillage the territory of the losing side. With modern times came a more civilized brand of warfare including the idea of reparations. However, the "Marshall Plan" that the United States initiated and implemented after World War II was unique in the history of warfare.

Two years after the end of World War II, the United States concluded that Western Europe would require substantial economic assistance to recover from the devastation of six years of war. In 1947, a plan, formally known as the European Recovery Program, was announced by then Secretary of State George C. Marshall.

The so-called Marshall Plan proposed that sixteen European countries draw up a unified plan for economic reconstruction to be funded by the United States. The

Soviet Union and other countries of Eastern Europe were invited to join, but they declined. The Economic Cooperation Administration was established by the United States to administer the plan. The sixteen West European countries then formed the Organization for European Economic Cooperation to coordinate the program.

For four years, from 1948 to 1952, the United States provided economic and technical assistance to the sixteen European countries. They received over thirteen billion dollars in American aid, the equivalent of more than sixty billion dollars today. The Marshall Plan was a great triumph, successfully accomplishing its goal of reviving the European economy and setting it on the path of long-term growth.

The tremendous success of the Marshall Plan has always been a source of pride and prestige for the American people. The Marshall Plan once again demonstrated the strength and proved the greatness of America. Not only was the United States the crucial factor in the defeat of Nazi Germany and the liberation of Europe, but once the war was over, America was instrumental in putting Europe back on the road to prosperity. America has a right to be proud of these accomplishments. On the other hand, black America is left to ponder how it had once again been overlooked, reluctant to ask questions for which there are no acceptable answers.

It is undoubtedly difficult for most black Americans to read about the Marshall Plan and not wonder why such a plan was never implemented for black America. The spirit and the purpose of the plan would be just as valid if the beneficiary of the plan were black America instead of Western Europe. The plan would be just as appropriate if the time and setting of the plan were "at the end of the Slavery era" or "at the end of the "Jim Crow era" instead of "at the end of World War II."

The cost of the Marshall Plan represents about two thousand dollars for every black American man, woman, and child. Certainly, a recovery plan of this magnitude for black America would produce the desired results. Along with history recording the success of the Marshall Plan, history could also record that "the black America recovery plan was a great triumph, successfully accomplishing its goal of establishing economic equality for black America."

Surely, if there were ever a people who deserve a Marshall Plan, it is black America. Many Europeans who were, in varying degrees, responsible for the outbreak of World War II benefited from the Marshal Plan. Many Europeans whose collaboration with the enemy helped to prolong the war also benefited from the Marshall Plan. A number of ex-Nazis even managed to find their way to America after the war was over.

On the other hand, black Americans certainly did nothing to contribute to their being the victims of three and a half centuries of Slavery and oppression. Yet, just a few weeks before the Marshall Plan was announced, white America was finally letting a black American play professional baseball after decades of restricting black players to their own segregated leagues. While white Americans were soberly mapping out plans to help Western Europe, other white Americans were cursing, throwing objects, and screaming racial epithets at Jackie Robinson.

Of course, white America can and does explain the rationale of the Marshall Plan as being what was best for America. The cold war with the Soviet Union was taking shape and Communism was a real threat to democracy in Europe. Restoring Western Europe's economy and stimulating trade among non-Communist countries was the best way to assure political stability in Europe. However, if this "what is best for America" explanation for the Marshall Plan is to be accepted, then there is another question to be answered. Is it best for America to allow a minority group that it has oppressed for centuries to remain as a permanent underclass in American society?

There are many black Americans who believe that white America is quite comfortable having a black underclass as a buffer to ensure that their own socioeconomic status in not easily lowered. These black Americans would argue that this is in fact the reason why there was a Marshall Plan for Western Europe and no such plan for black America. There are many black Americans who would remind us that Western Europe is white and the national origin of many white Americans. Finally, they would argue that, ultimately, race is a primary factor, if not the determining factor, when it comes to America helping those who are in need.

The good news for black America is that it is no longer important how true any of these arguments are. The only relevancy in discussing them is for purposes of inspiration and focus. Fortunately, black America is at a point in its history that it need not depend on white America to save it.

Black America's recovery plan must be initiated and implemented by black Americans. And when history records the "great triumph" of black America's recovery, it can also record that it was achieved by black Americans, for black Americans, once again "demonstrating the strength and proving the greatness of black America."

Affirmative Action Can Not Save Black America

Black Americans should be aware of the following ten items of information regarding affirmative action:

(1) Affirmative action has been described as "a formal effort to overcome past patterns of discrimination by providing increased employment opportunities for women and ethnic minorities."

(2) Affirmative action is such a controversial issue that virtually every aspect of it, including the seemingly benign description stated above, is subject to debate.

(3) The law that is the basis for affirmative action is the Equal Opportunity Act of 1972. This law affected most federal contractors and subcontractors, all state governments and institutions, including universities, and most local governments. The law required the initiation of plans to increase the proportions of female and minority employees until they were equal to the proportions existing in the available labor market.

(4) The measures employers and institutions have taken to demonstrate their compliance with the Equal Opportunity Act of 1972 have resulted in a multitude of court challenges and ultimately several Supreme Court decisions. In some cases, affirmative action measures have been upheld. In other cases, courts have ruled against affirmative action measures. To date, the most significant litigation involving affirmative action occurred in November of 1997. The United States Supreme Court refused to hear a challenge to a California law that ended all racial and gender preferences, thus clearing the way for other states and cities to ban affirmative action programs.

(5) Although most Americans are not familiar with the details of affirmative action, they believe they have a fundamental understanding of how it works. And, based on their perceptions, most people have made up their minds regarding the merits or lack of merits of affirmative action. In truth, to effectively argue the merits of affirmative action, one must become familiar with terms and concepts such as "equality of opportunity, equality of results, disparate treatment, disparate results, quotas, set-asides, goals, and timetables." One must also understand terms and concepts such as "preferential treatment, racial preferences, discrimination, reverse discrimination, collective responsibility, group remedy," and so forth. However, even after learning all there is to know

about affirmative action, very few Americans will ever change their original opinion of affirmative action.

(6) Some of the anecdotal arguments against affirmative action are: It is unequal and unfair treatment and therefore contrary to American laws, traditions, and values. Affirmative action punishes a selected group of present-day citizens for problems that occurred in the past, long before most of these citizens were born or before they or their ancestors came to the United States. One of the results of affirmative action is a lowering of standards and this is not what is best for America. Affirmative action is not the answer for minorities and women. The answer is to do what everyone else has done; work long and hard to be successful rather than waiting around to be handed success on a silver platter.

(7) Some of the anecdotal arguments for affirmative action are: It is no more unequal or unfair than the requirement of selected Americans to pay taxes that are used to support public schools or to wage war. Taxes are not based on which Americans use the public school system or which Americans are in favor of war. It is simply the price one must pay to live in a free, fair, democratic society. Affirmative action is akin to buying merchandise in good faith, or even receiving it free of charge, and it is later discovered

that the merchandise was stolen. The issue is not whether the new owner is being punished for the past sins of others, American laws, traditions, and values require that stolen property be returned to its rightful owner. Affirmative action results in diversity and diversity is good for America. Based on the numbers, there should be more affirmative action because the only thing that affirmative action has accomplished thus far is to prevent women and minorities from falling further behind.

(8) Affirmative action is, has always been, and will always be a racially divisive issue. This is the case even though it can easily be argued that women and the disabled have benefited as much or more than black Americans. Based on their perceptions, an overwhelming majority of black Americans strongly advocate affirmative action. Based on their perceptions, the majority of white Americans do not. This, of course, does not come as a surprise to most black Americans. They have four centuries of history to remind them that anything of benefit to black America will produce an automatic objection from most of white America.

(9) Affirmative action is another case of black Americans allowing themselves to believe, or to hope, that they will get their "forty acres and a mule." To date, black Americans have not received reparations and there is

no reason to believe that they ever will. Black Americans must operate under the assumption that, even after centuries of Slavery and oppression, the most they will ever get from white America is a fair and equal opportunity to do better in the future.

(10) Affirmative action can not save black America.

Of the ten items of information listed above, the most critical item for black Americans is that "affirmative action can not save black America." There are two major reasons why this is and will continue to be true.

Reason Number One

The most obvious reason why affirmative action can not save black America is because white America will never give affirmative action the opportunity to save black America. Most black Americans were skeptical from the beginning. Having a history filled with disappointments, a "wait and see attitude" made sense.

Many black Americans who were in the work force in the early seventies can vividly remember the company-wide announcements and the affirmative action meetings. If there was a consensus at the outset, it was that affirmative action would be largely ignored and eventually forgotten. After all, less than one hundred years earlier, white America had managed to successfully "ignore" both the 14th and 15th Amendments to the Constitution as well as four separate civil rights acts.

However, when it became apparent that affirmative action would not be ignored, white America, took another tack. They set about taking affirmative action apart; dismantling it nail by nail, board by board, floor by floor.

Black America should not be surprised by the timing of the California law that ended all racial and gender preferences. The Equal Opportunity Act of 1972 had been passed twenty-five years earlier by lawmakers who were graduating from law school just about the time that Jackie Robinson was breaking the major league baseball color barrier. These lawmakers and the Americans who elected them not only had first-hand knowledge of the Jim Crow era but they had also, on some level, benefited from it. During the past twenty-five years, the children of these Americans have grown up as eyewitnesses to "equal opportunity" for black Americans. They have no first-hand knowledge of the Jim Crow era and they see no reason why black Americans should be given any type of preferential treatment.

In the final analysis, affirmative action is all about black Americans getting their "forty acres and a mule." And when it comes to reparations, white America may agree in principle, but principles tend to disappear when it is time to pay for the land and the mules. The success of affirmative action depended on the benevolence of white America. That is, it was necessary for white Americans to want to make affirmative action work. Of course, not only did white America not give affirmative action its enthusiastic support, it barely gave affirmative action its reluctant cooperation. Instead, white America, as it has done in the past, began rounding up its mules and fencing in its acres.

Reason Number Two

The second reason why affirmative action can not save black America is because it was not designed to save black America. At best, the intention of affirmative action was to give black America a chance to save itself. In spite of arguments made by the most biased and partisan opponents of affirmative action, it was not created or designed to reward deficiency or incompetence. Affirmative action was designed to assist those who were "qualified" and, it can be argued, to help qualify those who were not.

Affirmative action never required colleges or universities to admit a specific number or percentage of black Americans regardless of their academic credentials. Affirmative action never required that employment be given to black Americans regardless of whether they could or could not perform the job. And there was certainly no affirmative action requirement to give a contract to someone to build a bridge or a building if that person was not qualified to build bridges or buildings.

Regardless of the job, designing a shopping center or hauling away its garbage, there was the requirement and expectation that it would be done by qualified individuals. How black Americans became "qualified" was ultimately the responsibility of black Americans. How black Americans become qualified will always be the responsibility of black Americans.

The bottom line is that black Americans will never receive reparations from white America for Slavery or Jim Crow era oppression. There will be no "forty acres and a mule," there will be no Marshall Plan, and affirmative action will eventually fade away. Even the idea of some manner of "official apology" by white America for Slavery has been rejected. On the one hand, black Americans are appalled that the idea of a simple apology even has to be debated. On the other hand, black Americans are primed to tell white America what it can do with its halfhearted, disingenuous, too little, too late apology.

The bottom line is that black America will never get more than "equal opportunity" from white America - the chance to play on a level playing field. Of course, the score was ninety-two to nine before white America decided that black America should not have to go two hundred yards to score a touchdown. But, white America has decided that what happened in the first three quarters of the game is not its problem. Because white America owns the ball, the playing field, and the referees the unfairness of the score is not white America's problem. It is indeed black America's problem.

The bottom line is that, at this point in black America's history, black Americans have two choices.

They can get mad or they can get even. Actually, black Americans do have a third choice. They can get mad and they can get even.

Michael Jordan Could Not Save Black America

During the four centuries that blacks have been in America, the measurement of their worth has been based almost exclusively on their physical abilities. The "best" male slaves were the ones who could pick the most cotton and the "best" female slaves were the ones who could deliver the most live births. Various personality traits were also important. The "best" slaves were docile, cooperative, and only as smart as they needed to be to pick cotton or to have babies.

Indeed, intelligent slaves were usually the most worrisome slaves. Aggression could be beaten out of most slaves and cooperation could often be beaten into them. On the other hand, an intelligent slave knew when to be docile, when to be cooperative, and also when to try to escape or to plan a slave revolt. This was, of course, one of the reasons it was illegal to educate slaves. White America clearly understood the connection between knowledge and power. White Americans absolutely understood that the continuation of Slavery depended on their ability to keep black Americans illiterate and as ignorant as possible.

Although educating black Americans was not illegal during the Jim Crow era, it certainly was not one of white America's priorities. And, unfortunately, it was usually not one of black America's highest priorities. Of course, black Americans had their hands full just trying to survive in a world where white Americans routinely did all that they could, legally and illegally, to try to keep black Americans "in their place." There is, however, another factor to be considered.

During two hundred and forty-six years of Slavery, white America declared that black Americans had no value except for their physical abilities. Not only did they say it, for twelve successive generations they demanded that black Americans accept as fact that they had no intellectual aptitude. How did this affect the mindset and even the psyche of black America? Did black Americans also come to measure their worth based primarily or solely on their physical abilities?

If this indeed was the mindset of black America after Slavery, the Jim Crow era did little to change it. Segregated black schools were vastly inferior to white schools, and because of the harsh lives that black Americans were forced to live, education was always secondary to day to day survival. Even for educated black Americans, opportunities were scarce in an American society characterized by racism and segregation. Still, there were a number of black American successes during the Jim Crow era. However, most of these successes, especially the ones that black

Americans heard about, were not successes as a result of intellectual pursuits. They were successes that were the result of the physical abilities of black Americans.

In 1908, Jack Johnson became the first black American to win the heavyweight boxing championship of the world. In 1974, Hank Aaron surpassed Babe Ruth's career home runs record. In between, there was Jesse Owens, Josh Gibson, Satchel Paige, Joe Louis, Jackie Robinson, Bob Beamom, and Willie Mays. The list also includes Bill Russell, Wilt Chamberlain, Jim Brown, Ernie Banks, Kareen Abdul-Jabbar, Muhammad Ali, and a host of other well-known black athletes.

Bert Williams, the first great black American entertainer, was making one hundred thousand dollars a year by 1915. In 1963, Sidney Poitier became the first black American actor to win an Academy Award. In between there was Lincoln Perry, Josephine Baker, Hattic McDaniel, Tim Moore, Cab Calloway, Duke Ellington, and Louis Armstrong. The list also includes Billie Holiday, Marian Anderson, Paul Robeson, Pearl Bailey, Della Reese, Nat King Cole, Ray Charles, and a host of other celebrated black entertainers.

There were, of course, black Americans during the Jim Crow era who made their mark on history outside of the sports and entertainment arena. However, if one is looking for celebrated successes in black America during the Jim Crow era, the overwhelming majority will be found in areas requiring physical ability rather than intellectual aptitude.

This premise can be tested by compiling a list of one hundred white Americans and a list of one hundred black Americans who were "famous," "influential," or were "role models" during the Jim Crow era. However, do not include the names of any sports and entertainment celebrities on either list. Of course, the list of white Americans could be compiled in a matter of minutes beginning with the twenty white men who served as president of the United States from 1866 through 1968. On the other hand, compiling the list of black Americans would require hours, if not days or weeks, of research by the average American.

How is this disparity to be explained? Is it the result of white America's expectation that black Americans can only excel in physical and not cerebral endeavors? Is it the result of black Americans buying into this notion after having it beaten into them for hundreds of years? Is it the result of Jim Crow era racism that limited opportunities for black Americans to only the sports and entertainment fields? Can the disparity be explained as a combination of these and other factors? Perhaps the only relevant question is, if a list were compiled of one hundred black American successes during the Equal Opportunity era that began in 1969, what would be the percentage of sports and entertainment celebrities on this list?

In fact, determining the answers to these questions is only important to the extent that doing so may help to dispel a myth that is largely a product of the Jim Crow era. The myth is that pursuing a career in professional sports or the entertainment field is an effective, viable, or even a reasonable way for black Americans to attain success in America.

Black America must immediately do all that it can to thoroughly destroy this myth. In the Slavery era or the Jim Crow era there may have been varying degrees of truth to this notion. However, in the Equal Opportunity era, attempting to use sports or entertainment as one's "ticket out of the ghetto" is a nonsensical proposition. In the Equal Opportunity era, it is more straightforward and infinitely easier for a black American to become a rich, successful physician than to become even a mediocre, lowly paid professional athlete or entertainer.

Hoop Dreams

For the 1996 – 1997 National Basketball Association season, the average salary was two million, two hundred thousand dollars with more than half of the players earning one million dollars or more. The minimum salary was two hundred and twenty thousand dollars for rookies and two hundred and forty-seven thousand dollars for veterans. More than ten percent of all NBA players earned four million dollars or more with the highest salary, a little more than thirty million dollars, being earned by Michael Jordan.

The financial rewards for playing professional basketball may be impressive but so are the rewards for winning a ten or twenty million dollar-lottery jackpot. In fact, the difficulty and probability factors are about the same.

First of all, with fifteen player positions on twenty-nine NBA teams, there is a maximum of four hundred and thirty-five professional basketball players in the NBA. Four hundred and thirty-five is also the number of members in the United States House of Representatives. Therefore, in terms of available job slots, it is just as easy to become a U.S. Representative as it is to make it to the NBA. Adding the one hundred U.S. Senators to the equation means that there are one hundred more available job slots in the U.S. Congress than in the NBA. In fact, a significantly larger number of people win a million dollars or more in state lotteries each year than the number of new player coming into the NBA each year.

Welcome To The NBA

After years of hard work and unwavering dedication, the final step to making it to the NBA is the annual draft of college players. In a sense, these athletes are very familiar with this selection process. Most of them were the first or second best players on their junior high school teams and were the only ones selected to play on their high school teams. Of the thousands of high schools with basketball programs, there are only a few very good teams. These are the teams that win most of their games, win their divisions, or win their state championships. Again, since there are many times more high schools than colleges, only the one or two best players from these teams are selected to play on college teams.

These "best of the best of the best" athletes make up the thousands of players who are eligible for the NBA draft each year. However, of these thousands of the best basketball players in America, only the best one hundred or so are even considered for employment by the NBA. Of these, only the best ten or so are deemed "can't miss" prospects and can expect to earn a lot more than the league minimum. In fact, after the twenty-nine teams have all made their first or second round selections in the draft, any other player selected is considered fortunate to even make the team. Those who do are lucky if they last with their team, or any team in the NBA, for more than a season or two.

Making it to the NBA is only half the battle. Staying in the NBA can be even more difficult. With the exception of the best three to six players on a team, players live with the very real possibility that they may not be re-signed when their contracts end. There is always the next annual draft and the influx of rookies desperate to make their mark and, of course, management is always looking to reduce costs by replacing the players they have with players who are just as good but with lower salary demands. Although the attention is usually on the superstars who play for ten or even fifteen years, this is not the norm. As a result of injuries, as a result of being replaced by younger and cheaper players, and as a result of just "losing a step," the average length of playing time in the NBA is about three years.

"Doctor J" versus Julius Irving, M.D.

Although making it to the NBA is largely a physical pursuit and becoming a physician is largely an intellectual pursuit, these two achievements have much in common. They both require a tremendous amount of dedication and an enormous amount of work. Anyone aspiring to play in the NBA must be prepared to spend two to four extra hours per day, everyday, practicing, conditioning, and learning all there is to know about basketball. Anyone aspiring to be a doctor must be prepared to spend two to four extra hours per day, everyday, reading, studying, and learning all there to know about medicine. It is a safe bet that many of the players who make it to the NBA, and many of those who do not, could have become physicians if that, instead of playing professional basketball, had been their goal.

Just as a goal of becoming a doctor and a goal of playing in the NBA have some things in common, there are also major differences. Perhaps the most significant difference is what happens to the small, by comparison, percentage of those who do not become doctors versus the incredibly high percentage of those who do not make it to the NBA.

Those who do not achieve their ultimate goal of becoming physicians, almost always graduate from college with a quality education. Because they were already in medical school or had planned to attend medical school, the idea of earning an advanced degree is already firmly established in their minds. Almost all "medical school dropouts" find rewarding, challenging, well-paying jobs in the field of medicine or elsewhere.

Those who do not achieve their ultimate goal to play in the NBA do not fair nearly as well. Some flunk out or leave college long before they graduate. Others, having been pushed through the system because of their athletic ability, are not prepared to meet the challenges they must face when basketball is no longer their claim to fame. One will never find a forty year-old black man with a mediocre job, sitting around a neighborhood barbershop, telling stories of how good he was in college and explaining that if it were not for a bad knee, he would have become a physician or an attorney.

Another significant difference between playing in the NBA and becoming a physician is that, if one successfully completes medical school, one can become a doctor. This is the reason why there are eight hundred thousand physicians in America. With only four hundred and thirty-five jobs in the NBA, one can be the five hundredth best basketball player in America and not even come close to making it to the NBA.

Of course, the difference between physicians and NBA players that most people tend to focus on is the difference in salaries. However, they also tend to overlook or downplay the most obvious obstacle. In order to earn a multi-million dollar NBA salary, one must first get to the NBA. And, while it may be difficult to become a doctor, the odds of making it to the NBA are astronomical. Attempting to become a physician is a goal. Attempting to become a player in the NBA is, at best, a million-to-one gamble. And, again, just making it to the NBA is no guarantee of financial success. Only a handful of superstars receive multi-million dollar, multi-year contracts.

There is one additional consideration that is often overlooked when comparing the salaries of doctors, lawyers, and other professionals versus the salaries of professional athletes. The average annual salary of a NBA player is more than two million dollars. The average annual salary of a physician is two hundred thousand dollars. This difference may seem significant until one considers the average length of an NBA career versus the likelihood of a doctor practicing medicine for twenty, thirty, or forty years. It is this lifetime earning potential that also makes the high cost of medical school a worthwhile investment for anyone's future.

In any discussion of physical endeavors versus intellectual pursuits it must be acknowledged that the lines between the two are not always so clearly drawn. Becoming a doctor, a lawyer, an engineer, or an accountant is physically demanding. And becoming a football player, a rap singer, or a ballet dancer requires intelligence on many levels. In fact, the most successful athletes and entertainers are usually the ones who possess a balanced combination of talent and intelligence.

This was certainly the case for the black entertainers and athletes who were successful during the Jim Crow era. They are to be greatly admired for having the talent and the intelligence to be successful at a time when white Americans cringed at the success of any black American. And they are certainly to be honored for what they accomplished. Their achievements, as much as any other factor, helped to bring an end to the Jim Crow era.

However, in spite of the great contributions that black athletes and entertainers have made in the past and will continue to make in the future, sports and entertainment can not save black America. Michael Jordan, as a superstar basketball player, as one of the best athletes and best entertainers in American history, could not save black America. Indeed, five or ten new Michael Jordans can not save black America.

Who can save black America? Tens of thousands more black CEO's and company presidents can save black America. Tens of thousands more black judges and attorneys can save black America. Tens of thousands more black physicians and other medical professionals can save black America. Tens of thousands more black engineers and architects can save black America. Tens of thousands more black accountants and data processing professionals can save black America. And, in fact, it would be easier for black America to produce these hundreds of thousands of black professionals than it would be for black America to produce another five or ten Michael Jordans.

Michael Jordan, the superstar basketball player, could not save black America. However, Michael Jordan, the black American, hero and role model to millions of black youths, can help to save black America. He can begin by telling all the black youths who "want to be like Mike" what it actually means to be like Mike.

To be like Mike is to understand that there are no short cuts in life, that hard work is the only way to be successful, and that everyone has to pay his or her dues. To be like Mike is to stay out of trouble, stay off drugs, and always be strong enough to do the right thing. To be like Mike is to make goals, set objectives, and to be focused and persistent enough to accomplish them. And, most importantly, to be like Mike is to be an intelligent, articulate, college graduate.

To be like Mike may mean being a great basketball player for one black youth out of a million. The goal of black America must be to determine and maximize the innate talents of the other nine hundred and ninety-nine thousand black youths. Black America will have learned this lesson when more twelve-year old black youths respond to questions about their future by answering: "I want to be like Mike. I want to do medical research when I grow up and discover a cure for sickle-cell disease."

Black America Must Accept That It Needs To Be "Saved"

Based on all standard economic measurements and social indicators, black America's socioeconomic standing is remarkably lower than the socioeconomic standing of white America. Compared to all other racial and ethnic minorities, black America is at or near the bottom of every social and economic category.

Black Population

Year	Total Black Americans	Percent of Population
1619	20	2.5%
1790	758,000	19.3%
1850	3,641,000	15.7%
1900	8,815,000	11.6%
1930	11,909,000	9.7%
1940	12,904,000	9.8%
1960	18,795,000	10.5%
1970	22,567,000	11.1%
1990	30,592,000	12.3%
1996	33,900,000	12.8%

Family and Health

A majority of all black American children live in single parent homes. About half of all black American children are reared by single black females.

Family Structure (1991)	Black Families	White Families
Married Couples	46.1%	82.8%
Female Householder	46.8%	12.4%
Male Householder	7.1%	4.3%

Teenage mothers give birth to one-fifth of all black children.

Pregnancies (1991)	Black Americans	White Americans
Total	1,344,000	4,929,000
Teenagers (19 and Under)	286,000	678,000
Percent Teenager	21.3%	13.8%

Fetal, neonatal, and infant mortality rates are higher for black Americans than white Americans.

Although black Americans are less than thirteen percent of the population, they account for more than one-third of all abortions.

Abortions (1991)	Black Americans	White Americans
Total	574,000	982,000
Percent	37%	63%

The percentage of black Americans who die as a result of firearms, drug-induced causes, and alcohol-induced causes is greater than the percentage of white Americans who die from these same causes.

Although black Americans are less than thirteen percent of the population, they account for over one-third of all AIDS deaths.

The life expectancy of black males is remarkably shorter than the life expectancy of all other Americans.

Number Years Life Expectancy At Birth				
Year	Black Male	White Male	Black Female	White Female
1970	60.0	68.0	68.3	75.6
1982	65.1	71.5	73.6	78.7
1994	64.9	73.2	74.1	79.6

Employment and Income

The lack of gainful employment has historically been a problem within black America. In recent years, Census Bureau data has indicated that black unemployment is approximately three times greater than white unemployment. However, it has been argued that this data does not reflect the many black Americans who have become discouraged and given up looking for employment or the large number of black Americans who are under-employed. Because of these and other factors, it is often argued that up to six times more black Americans than white Americans are unemployed and under-employed.

Unemployment (1996)	Black Americans	White Americans
Total Persons	11.6%	4.6%
Males, 16 and Over	14.2%	5.1%
Females, 16 and Over	9.2%	3.9%

Unemployment and under-employment are two of the reasons median income is lower for black Americans than it is for white Americans in all income categories.

The median income in 1995 for black families headed by a female, with no spouse present, was $15,004. Black families headed by a female, with no spouse present, account for almost half of all black families.

Median Income (1995)	Black Americans	White Americans
Individual Full-Time Workers	$22,470	$30,815
Families (All types)	$25,970	$45,020
Families/Female Householder	$15,004	$24,467

A greater percentage of black Americans are on welfare than any other racial or ethnic group in America.

Eleven of every one hundred white children live in poverty. Forty-two of every one hundred black children live in poverty.

Living Below The Poverty Income Level (1995)	Black Americans	White Americans
Total Persons	29.3%	8.5%
Males	25.7%	7.4%
Females	32.4%	9.6%
All Families	26.4%	6.4%
Families/Female Householder	45.1%	21.5%
Children (Under 18)	41.9%	11.2%

Crime and Criminal Justice

Black Americans, based on percentage of population, are more likely to be victims of all types of crimes: murder, negligent manslaughter, forcible rape, robbery, aggravated assault, burglary, larceny, and motor vehicle theft.

There are more black Americans, based on percentage of population, who are in federal and state prisons and local jails. There are also more black Americans who are on parole and more black Americans who are on death row.

Although black Americans are only one eighth of the population, more than one half of all murder victims are black Americans.

All Murder Victims (1994)	Black Americans	White Americans
Total	11,223	10,198
Percent	50.8%	46.2%

Black America Must Be Saved

Black Americans must accept that black America needs to be saved. Black Americans must understand that only they can save black America.

Only Black Americans Can Save Black America

Only black Americans can save black America. The message is clear and concise and the meaning seems obvious. And who could argue against the logic and appropriateness of black Americans being responsible for their own fate? However, there is more to be said and understood about this seemingly simple statement of fact.

To begin with, "only black Americans can save black America" is more than a catchy slogan. It is one of the most critical issues that black Americans must acknowledge, examine, and resolve as a prerequisite to improving their socioeconomic standing in America. The statement itself answers the question, "who" can save black America. The "what" in the statement is saving black Americans from, at a minimum, another one hundred years of having the lowest socioeconomic standing in America. The "how" is addressed in many of the other "Project 2019 Issues." It is "why" only black Americans can save black America that is to be considered and examined here.

"Why" can only black Americans save black America? There are a number of possible ways to answer this question as well as a number of possible answers. However, the single best answer to why only black Americans can save black America is, ultimately, because only black Americans truly care if black America is saved. This answer may seem a bit harsh and perhaps it is. Even so, the answer is not meant to suggest that all white Americans are hardened racists who have absolutely no sympathy for the plight of millions of black Americans. Nor is the answer meant in any way to insult or disparage the many white Americans who have fought and died in the struggle for freedom and civil rights for black Americans. Yet, in the grand scheme of things, as well as on the most basic level, only black Americans have a vested interest in black America being saved.

Some people in America and many people around the world sincerely believe that America is a vile, evil nation that represents all that is wrong with the world. Other people will risk their lives or prostitute themselves to become American citizens. White Americans are alternately described as being noble, generous, and compassionate and as being contemptible, greedy, and hardhearted. But, whatever else white Americans are, they are human.

Being human, white Americans are governed, or at a minimum guided, by instincts. It is this instinctual behavior that has led humans to populate every corner of this world and to look to the stars for other challenges. Of all human instincts, the instinct for survival of the human species is by far the strongest. For any given human, self-preservation is at the top of this list. For this same human, his or her child almost always has at least an equally high priority. Humans will kill or be killed protecting the lives of their children. The instinct for survival also extends to loved ones, it extends to close family members, and it extends to more distant family members. However, it does not stop there. And where it goes next says a lot about a person or explains a great deal about a people.

Anyone can quickly determine the direction in which their humanity flows after having ensured their own personal survival. Here is a test: God has selected all the people who truly deserve to go to heaven and there is still a lot of room left. You are put in charge of filling the remaining space and you are given two minutes to complete the task. And, of course, when heaven is full, or when the two minutes are up, all those not selected are condemned to a sea of fire and brimstone waiting in hell below.

After making sure that your immediate family, other relatives, and just about everyone that you personally know are sent to heaven, who do you select next? God has already made all of the obvious selections like "all of the innocent children," and "all the virtuous and righteous people regardless of their faith." He has also already condemned all the truly evil people to hell.

Is your next selection all the people of your religion who have not yet been chosen? Do you select all the people of your nationality or culture who have not yet been chosen? Do you select all of the Democrats or all of the Republicans, all of the liberals or all of the conservatives? There would, of course, be a loud groan of disapproval if the first selection of a racist were all the people of his or her race who had not yet been chosen. On the other hand, what if the person choosing was down to his or her last couple of selections? Is there any doubt, that if you had not yet been chosen, that you would be desperately hoping that you and the person doing the selecting were the same race?

It is human nature for people to care more about those close to them than to care about those who are not. This is the case whether stepping in front of a bullet to protect one's child, being asked to donate a kidney to a sibling, or hiring a cousin to work in one's office. And although selecting who gets into heaven and saving black America are not in the same category, the same survival instincts apply. White Americans may be willing to help save black America, but only after they have saved their families, after they have saved their loved ones, after they have saved their friends, after they have saved all the people of their ethnic group, and so forth.

Clearly, if black Americans do not save black America then black America will never be saved. First and foremost, only black Americans have a vested interest in saving black America. Additionally, all the crucial elements necessary to save black America must come from black America. Only black Americans can do the extensive, arduous work that is necessary to save black America. Only black Americans can make the

126

sacrifices that are necessary to save black America. Only black Americans will ever have a compelling desire to save black America.   If black America is ultimately saved, it will be saved by black Americans.

How To Succeed In America The Land Of Opportunity

Although the so-called "American Dream" is promised to all Americans, it has often been defined in terms of those who have come to America in search of the dream. In the beginning, the American Dream meant a choice of how to worship one's God without paying for that choice with a lifetime of persecution. Later, the promise of financial success was so great that it was said that the streets of America were paved with gold. In a few cases, huge fortunes were made as a result of being the first to discover a stream laden with gold or by being fortunate enough to buy a piece of property with rich oil reserves.

For some people, the American Dream is about freedom, justice, or personal dignity and it has little or nothing to do with wealth or social standing. For many people, the American Dream is living upper middle-class lives on small family farms or in quiet suburban neighborhoods. For everyone, the American Dream is about the opportunity to succeed in one's own personal pursuit of happiness.

Regardless of one's version of the American Dream, it has always been understood and accepted how the dream was to be obtained. It had to be earned. Simply immigrating to America, or even being born in America, was never a guarantee of success. From the beginning, there was a price that had to be paid. In general, the requirements for success in America have not really changed very much over the years. However, for black Americans, the requirements for success in America have changed dramatically.

Historical Requirements For Success In America
    Three hundred, one hundred, or even fifty years ago, a list of requirements for success in America would have included hard work, dedication, resourcefulness, and knowledge. Self-motivation, good health, intelligence, imagination, inventiveness, and courage could also be included on the list. And, of course, until the Civil Rights victories of the 1950's and 1960's, being white was a major requirement for being successful in America.
    Of the historical requirements for white Americans to obtain the American Dream, the most important were hard work and dedication. It did not matter if one was a rancher or a farmer, a blacksmith or a cobbler, a factory worker or a small business owner, the formula was the same. "Get up early every morning. Work as hard as you can. Put in as many hours as possible. Spend your dollars wisely. And save every penny you can."
    This formula almost always worked to perfection. Over a period of five or ten years, one would have saved enough money for a down payment on a decent

bungalow in a respectable part of town. Over a period of ten or fifteen years, one would have accumulated the resources to add another sixty acres of land to the family farm. Over a period of fifteen or twenty years, one would have enough capital to start the business that he or she had always dreamed of owning.

It is notable that, in the past, this formula for success was not adversely affected by one's lack of "formal education." Indeed, for most of America's history, a formal education would not have been high on most lists of requirements for success in America.

This should not come as a surprise to most Americans given the way that American history is usually presented or portrayed. Only occasionally, somewhere between the big gunfight and the cavalry rescuing the wagon train, is there a scene of a sweet, pretty schoolmarm teaching young children to read and write. There are also the bigger than life examples of men like Cornelius Vanderbilt, Jay Gould, and John Rockefeller; self-made men who, with little or no formal education, amassed incredible fortunes.

Statistics confirm that, in the past, formal education was not a requirement for success in America. Today, more than eight of every ten Americans complete high school. As late as 1940, less than one fourth of all Americans completed high school. Today, almost one fourth of Americans complete at least four years of college. In 1940, less than five percent completed four years of college. Based on these statistics, one could conclude that, for most of America's history, being able to read and write was the only educational requirement for success.

For most of America's history, life was a lot less complicated than it is as we approach the twenty-first century. America was largely an agrarian society and much of the science and technology that is now taught in our schools had not yet even been developed. Even with the industrial revolution of the nineteenth century, America did not change from a largely agrarian society into an industrial urban society until well into the twentieth century. The last major rural decline occurred from 1950 to 1980. Even as the United States farm output doubled during this period, the number of farms fell from five and a half million to two and a half million and the farm population shrank from fifteen percent to less than three percent of the total population.

Clearly, the primary and secondary formal education that is now mandatory in the United States was not always necessary for success in America. However, it must be stated just as clearly that "knowledge" has always been a requirement for success in America. This was just as true in 1900, 1800, and 1700 as it is today.

The difference is not the requirement of knowledge. The difference is how the knowledge is acquired. Prior to the technical revolution of the latter half of the twentieth century, a formal education was rarely the best way for most Americans to obtain the knowledge that was required for success. In fact, for much of America's history, it would have been counter-productive to have healthy young men and women sitting around in classrooms until they were eighteen years old.

In the past, young Americans obtained the knowledge and developed the skills that were necessary for them to succeed largely from formal apprenticeship programs and informal apprenticeship situations. This was the case both for agricultural endeavors as well as for the trades and crafts that dominated urban areas. On-the-job training was how one learned from their father to be a good farmer, rancher, or blacksmith. On-the-job training was how one learned from a master to be a good cobbler, bricklayer, or plumber.

Although hard work and dedication have always been essential for success in America, hard work and dedication are pointless without the knowledge and skill to do quality, profitable work. This was just as true for settlers, trappers, and gold prospectors as it was for the Vanderbilts, the Goulds, and the Rockefellers.

21st Century Requirements For Success In America

Much of what was required in the past to be successful in America still applies today. The good news for black America is that being white is no longer a major requirement for being successful. The bad news for black America is that having a quality formal education is now a major requirement for success in America.

Working hard, knowledge, resourcefulness, and dedication are still essential elements for success in

America. And, as we enter the extraordinary world of the twenty-first century, creativity, imagination, and inventiveness will become more and more critical to success. However, there is no doubt that the most dramatic change that has occurred in the quest of the American Dream is how knowledge is obtained. In the twenty-first century, the knowledge and skills that will be required to succeed in America can best, and in most cases can only, be acquired as a result of formal education.

An early indication that America's leadership understood this to be the case was the passage of the Servicemen's Readjustment Act by Congress in 1944. It was the first of a series of programs that would become popularly known as the G.I. Bill of Rights. These programs would ultimately provide educational and economic assistance to veterans of World War II, the Korean War, and the Vietnam War.

It would seem that veterans understood the necessity of education as the educational benefits proved to be the most popular part of the G.I. Bill of Rights. Almost eight million veterans of World War II took advantage of the educational provisions. To date, well over twenty million veterans of three wars had received training or educational assistance under the various G.I. Bills. For some black veterans, this educational assistance helped them to become the first members of their families to earn college degrees.

Since it was founded, America, more so than any other nation, has been a country where fully franchised citizens have a genuine opportunity to achieve success and happiness. In the past, all that was required was hard work and the desire to succeed: the so-called American work ethic.

Surely, the American work ethic is ingrained in black America. For almost four centuries now, millions of black Americans have gotten up every morning and worked as hard as they could. The problem is that, for most of these four centuries, black Americans have not had the knowledge or skills to engage in quality, profitable work. The end results of black Americans being slaves in 1850 and black Americans working in fast-food restaurants in 1999 are exactly the same. They receive the minimum amount of food and shelter that will enable them to work yet another day.

The lesson that black Americans must learn is that they must apply their work ethic to obtaining knowledge. Black Americans must work long and hard to get a quality formal education before they enter the work force rather than simply working hard after they enter the work force. If they did, they would no longer be relegated to spending their lives working from dawn to dusk to make white America successful. If they did, their hard work would lead to their own success and the success of black America. For black Americans, the problem is not about working harder, it is in fact all about working smarter.

"Knowledge Is Power"

Conservative philosophers of education tend to view education mainly as a "product," the end results of teaching and learning activities. They focus on factors such as goals, aims, competence, effective teaching, and standards. Progressive philosophers of education tend to view education as being a "process." They are primarily concerned with the quality of the learner's experience, the nature of methodologies, the relationships between teachers and students, and the relationships among students. Others argue that product and process are more or less inseparable.

While there may be philosophical differences regarding the purposes, policies, and practices of education, it is generally agreed that assimilating "knowledge" is the primary function of education. Even so, there are different philosophies of what constitutes knowledge, a distinction being made between "knowing how" and "knowing that." Again, an argument can be made that the two are inseparable. In any case, the end results of "knowing" will always be the same. The product of knowledge is power.

The aphorism "knowledge is power" is ascribed to noted sixteenth century English statesman, essayist, and philosopher, Sir Francis Bacon. Almost certainly, he was not the first person to use these three succinct words to so elegantly express this most fundamental truth. Without any doubt, he was not the first human to realize that knowledge is the source of all genuine, meaningful power.

The Intellectual Ascent Of Humankind

Based solely on physiology, Homo sapiens are far from what is usually deemed to be a magnificent species. Humans certainly have never possessed the physical attributes usually associated with many highly successful species. Humans are not very fast, they are not very big, they are not very strong, and they are not especially ferocious. Most mammals can see better, can hear better, and have a much more acute sense of smell.

Humans are not poisonous, they can not change colors to match their surroundings, and they can live only a few days without food and water. Humans cannot fly, they can not live on both land and water, and even their ability to scurry up trees was lost somewhere in their distant past. The physical attributes that humans have always possessed were, at best, adequate to survive as a species. Humans, however, have done much, much more than just survive. They have become the masters and rulers of their world.

Thousands of years ago, our primeval ancestors had to worry about being hunted into extinction by predatory animals on the African Savannah. Today, humans routinely cause the extinction of entire species of animals for sport, profit, or in the name of progress. The last species to so completely dominate the Earth were the dinosaurs. For more than one hundred million years, they ruled as a result of their size, strength, ferocity, and numbers. However, the power that humans now use to rule their world is not based on size or strength or any other physical attribute. Humans became and remain masters of the Earth as a result of the power of the human brain.

Humans could have never out-muscled, out-hunted, and certainly not outrun the rest of the animal kingdom. Thankfully, they were destined to become the most intelligent animals on earth. If it were not for the development of their most powerful weapon, the human brain, humans certainly would have never distinguished themselves as a species. Indeed, like millions of other species, they might well be extinct by now. Instead, over the last few hundred thousand years, their intelligence has allowed them to accomplish feats that no other animal, in hundreds and hundreds of millions of years, has had the intelligence to accomplish.

The Power Of Knowledge

As a result of one of their first and most significant achievements in logic and reasoning, humans learned to control and use fire. All that humans have done since could not have been accomplished without this one paramount step. Before humans learned to use fire, they had no single skill that significantly distinguished them from any other animal on Earth.

It was their use of fire that separated humans from the rest of the animal kingdom and helped to ensure their survival as a species. However, it was their ability to use simple tools to create fire that was and remains the single greatest technological achievement of humankind. Learning to create fire catapulted humans into the position to become the masters and rulers of the Earth. It would accelerate their development more so than any other factor in their history. Even today, humans still use the fire of their bombs to conquer other humans and the fire of their rockets to take humans to the moon and beyond.

Humans using their own tools to create fire was only the beginning. While other animals have mastered the use of simple tools, with the use of fire, humans were able to make more tools, better tools, and more complex tools. With their discovery of cultivation, humans quickly began down the road that would lead them to civilization. By the time humans developed the wheel and the plow, they were well on their way to using knowledge to conquer their world.

Humans, however, were not satisfied with just conquering their environment. They were not satisfied with simply establishing dominance over the rest of the animal kingdom. Humans began to use their knowledge to conquer other human beings. Thousands of years before the birth of Christ, humans began creating great civilizations, city-states, kingdoms, and empires: Sumer, Mesopotamia, Babylonia, Assyria, Egypt, Persia, and eventually the Roman Empire.

These ancient empires were not created and did not last for hundreds of years by virtue of rampaging hordes and brute force. These empires were successful because of the power of knowledge. These humans understood planning and logistics and they knew how to move and how to feed great armies. They learned how to build better weapons then their enemies and how to use the stars to navigate their ships. The success of these empires was the result of knowing how to govern and rule effectively, even from hundreds or thousands of miles away. It was knowledge that accounts for the success of the great empires of the past. It is knowledge that accounts for the "empires" that exist in the world today.

The Power Of Education: In The Beginning

Over the course of human history, the success of the human species has depended on its ability to preserve its ever-increasing wealth of accumulated knowledge. The challenge has always been for humans to successfully disseminate knowledge to their children, for their children to successfully assimilate that knowledge, and for them to eventually pass it on to their children. In the earliest history of humankind, as with most species, children learned from their parents and other family members how to survive in a hostile environment. They learned the best foods to eat, what foods not to eat, and how to themselves avoid becoming a meal. Such informal education is just as important today. Parents must teach their children to avoid drugs, casual sex, and other equally dangerous pitfalls of our modern world.

Throughout recorded history societies have used formal education to disseminate knowledge to those who will succeed them. According to Chinese history, the "Hundred Schools of thought" was established around 1000 BC for rulers and nobles. Four hundred years later, formal education was widely available in China to officials and members of the wealthier classes. The "Academy" was established by Plato, Socrates' disciple, in about 387 BC. It is considered to have been one of the world's first universities. "Lyceum," a similar type of university, was founded by Aristotle in 335 BC. In Roman schools, boys were given a general education that included the study of literature, linguistics, astronomy, geometry, music, logic, history, and philosophy.

During the Middle Ages, which began with the fall of Rome in AD 476, research centers and universities flourished in Baghdad, Cairo, Alexandria, Cordoba, and other Islamic cities. In Western Europe, during their so-called "Dark Ages," very little progress was made in education. Most of the formal education of the period was religious in nature and was provided by monasteries in Ireland and northern England. However, beginning in the eleventh century, renowned universities and colleges such as the University of Paris, the Sorbonne, Oxford, and Cambridge were founded.

Long before the fifteenth century, humans had already achieved the two most significant requirements for disseminating and assimilating knowledge. They had developed spoken language and they had created written language. The third most significant achievement occurred as a result of successfully using movable type for printing. With this development, it was finally possible to economically publish books in large quantities, making knowledge on a variety of subjects available to even the common man.

The Power Of Education: For The Masses

The availability of printed material would lead to broader patterns of education and would help drive the Renaissance, the cultural and intellectual movement that had begun in the fourteenth century. Leaders of the Protestant Reformation believed that it was important for all Christians to read the Bible and they urged the establishment of national education systems. During this same period, the Jesuits began establishing schools throughout Europe and a century later the Christian Brothers would establish an extensive system of Catholic schools for the poor. This period was also the era of the great scientific theories and discoveries of Copernicus, Galileo, Kepler, and Newton.

During the seventeenth century, men such as Francis Bacon and John Locke emerged to encourage the scientific revolution of the times and to argue that the advancement of knowledge was beneficial to human society in general. Also, during the seventeenth century, the earliest American colleges, Harvard, Yale, and William and Mary were founded. By the eighteenth century, the basic foundations of many national educational systems had begun to develop. And, during the nineteenth century, many national school systems began to assume their modern form.

In the twentieth century, particularly after World War II, American politicians and educators renewed efforts to provide a high-quality general academic education for America's children. Also in the twentieth century, the proliferation of colleges, universities, and special institutes has made higher education available to many more Americans. Finally, in recent years, the numbers of junior colleges, community colleges, and vocational schools have been increased in order to educate Americans who are unable to attend more traditional four-year colleges. These schools also enable adults to pursue topics of interests or to begin working towards different careers.

As the twentieth century comes to an end, there is a very good reason why America spends billions of dollars on education each year and Americans are only marginally satisfied with the results. There is a very good reason why more than eight out every ten

Americans complete high school and America thinks that it can and should do better. There is a very good reason why more than one out of every five Americans earns a college degree and America believes that it is not enough. The reason is that America is the most powerful nation on Earth and Americans want to keep it that way.

In the twenty-first century, education and knowledge will be important to America for all the predictable reasons. Seeking knowledge is an innate part of the human spirit. Competition among developed countries is increasing and even developing countries are beginning to eradicate illiteracy. Additional knowledge is needed to solve the problems of a world that continuously increases in complexity.

Beyond the expected reasons, there will also be a need for the knowledge to help humankind deal with the place where knowledge has taken it. As a result of incredible knowledge, humankind has developed incredible power, including the power to destroy our world on many different levels. In the twenty-first century, humankind will need to gain the wisdom to use such incredible power for the benefit and not to the detriment of humankind.

How To Enslave A People

In order to understand how and why knowledge is power, one must understand the meaning and the nature of "power." Power is defined as "the ability to act or produce an effect," "possession of control, authority, or influence over others," and "physical might." One of the most classic examples of the use of power was Slavery. However, most black Americans do not fully understand or appreciate the nature of the power that was used to enslave their ancestors. Most black Americans are under the impression that the success of Slavery was the result of power as defined by "physical might," that slaves were whipped and beaten into submission. Nothing could be further from the truth.

When the Declaration of Independence was being signed, black Americans comprised approximately twenty percent of the total population of the colonies. The Russian Revolution, by contrast, was accomplished by about ten percent of the Russian population. During Slavery, in many counties in the Deep South, the slave population exceeded the white population by more than two to one. In a few counties, slaves outnumbered whites by as many as ten to one.

By 1860, more than three-fourths of all slaves lived on plantations and on some of the larger plantations they outnumbered whites by as many as one hundred to one. Also, during this time, the total population of slave states consisted of eight million whites and four million blacks. Yet, there were relatively few slave revolts. Those that began were quickly put down and the vast majority of them never got past the "conspiracy" stage. One of the reasons for these failures was the high incident of "betrayal" by other slaves to their white masters.

If Slavery were only about "physical might," then black Americans would have had a much better chance of mounting a successful revolt. However, the success of Slavery was the result of the other definition of power: "possession of control, authority, or influence over others." The control, the authority, and the influence that whites had over blacks were not accomplished as a result of physical power but rather psychological power. In two hundred and forty-six years of Slavery, white Americans assimilated the knowledge required to enslave a people and they passed it down from generation to generation in the form of discourses, pamphlets, and other publications.

Although there were variations, the basic tenets used to train an "ideal slave" included:
- A master should implant within his slave's mind and continuously remind him of his innate inferiority. He is less than human, his African ancestors are only a small step above apes, his dark color is a badge of degradation, and according to the laws of God and the laws of nature he was put on earth to be a slave. Even as an adult, he is a "boy" and his wife is a "girl."
- A master should implant within his slave's mind and continuously remind him of his helplessness and dependency on his master. Even as an adult, he is merely a child that would not survive without the benevolence of his master.

- A master should awe his slave with a sense of his enormous power and implant within the slave's mind a paralyzing fear of white men. The only reason his master has to not beat him to death is that he continues to serve his master faithfully.
- A master should convince his slave that the master's success is also his success and the master's failure is also his failure. A master might reward a female with a new dress for delivering a healthy infant slave.
- A master must maintain strict discipline at all times. A master must require unconditional submission. His slave is not for a single moment to exercise his will or judgement in opposition to his master's orders.

Of course, physical might was used. Slaves were whipped, beaten, mutilated, and otherwise physically abused. However, doing so was rarely what the owner of a slave wanted to do but rather what he felt he needed to do. First of all, physical abuse was counter-productive. A severely beaten or injured slave could not work and the death of a slave was a direct financial loss to the slave's owner. Secondly, having to beat a slave was to an extent an admission or at least an indication that no matter how well a slave was trained, Slavery was not the natural order of the universe.

While physical might was used, make no mistake, the physical power that was exerted over slaves was secondary, used only to reinforce the psychological control that was the real power used to subjugate slaves.

148

This explains why dozens of "physically powerful" black men would stand around watching "powerlessly" as one of their relatives or friends was beaten like an animal by a lone white man. This is also the reason some slaves would betray other slaves who were conspiring to start a revolt. Those doing the betraying truly believed that such an uprising would lead to the "ruination" of them all. If physical power had to be used a lot, it was because many blacks Americans never completely bought into the slave owners psychological terrorism and attempt at mind control.

Slavery was a success not only because white Americans were in possession of knowledge that gave them power. An equally important element was the inherent weaknesses of black Americans as a result of their lack of knowledge. Policies were established, slaves codes were written, and laws were enacted to ensure that slaves were not educated, could not assemble, and had no way of mass communicating.

In order for Slavery to endure, slaves needed to be kept ignorant about the world beyond their plantation and ignorant about life in general. Many had no real knowledge of how to survive once off of their plantation. Unlike Native Americans who the early colonists had tried and failed to enslave, America was a foreign land to even those black Americans who had lived their entire lives in America.

Understanding And Recognizing Real Power

Clearly, black Americans have not learned that physical power is no match for intellectual power. Perhaps this is the result of black Americans having been conditioned over the centuries to think of power in a narrow, limited fashion. During Slavery, they only saw the physical power that was wielded against them. In their ignorance, they could not understand the psychological power that was being used against them. Also, since blacks have been in America, they have been valued only for their physical power and physical abilities. Perhaps this helps to explain black Americans lack of understanding of the true nature of power.

Somewhere in America, a thirty year-old black gang leader is watching a basketball game on television. He is a high school dropout. He never worked hard to get good grades because he had visions of playing professional basketball or hopes that the rap group he and his friends started would eventually take off. He puts down the joint he is smoking and picks up his Glock 19, 9mm, semi-automatic handgun that is his constant companion. Fondling it, he marvels at what a powerful weapon it is and how just having it gets him a lot of respect. With his Glock, the man has the power to control the powerless people around him through fear and intimidation. However, his lifestyle and the type of behavior that the man must exhibit to maintain his power means that he is always in imminent danger of death or incarceration. In fact, this black man has about as much power as his great-great-great grandfather had on the plantation where he lived as a slave until he died.

Somewhere in America, there is a thirty year-old white man watching the same basketball game. However, he is watching the game from floor seats at the stadium where the game is being played. He worked hard in high school, did homework and studied in the evenings, and he received excellent grades. He then went to college, worked hard, and earned a bachelor's degree. While working at a full-time job, he went to school in the evenings to get an MBA. Within the next few years, his salary will be close to one hundred thousand dollars a year. In fact, he is an executive at a company that imports and sells Glock handguns. He does not own a Glock or any other gun because he lives in a neighborhood with such a low crime rate that it is even safe for him to go jogging in the evenings. He knows lawyers, accountants, and bankers and he is developing relationships with local politicians. He is a man with real power.

Black Americans must understand that physical might is the least effective kind of power and that it has been declining in importance since the human intellect began to develop. The most successful early humans were the ones who first learned how to control and use fire. Those who learned to create fire were even more successful. Humans who made tools using metal succeeded over those who did not. Humans who first used gunpowder in their weapons easily conquered those who did not.

Today, the most successful nations are the nations that are the most technically advanced. The United States is not the most successful and powerful nation in the world simply because it is a free and open democracy. It is the most powerful nation on earth because our capitalistic system is designed to generously reward those who come up with the best and the brightest ideas.

If black Americans are to succeed in America, they must understand the nature of power. If black Americans are to succeed in America, they must accept that power is a product of knowledge. If black Americans are to succeed in America, they must acquire knowledge through formal education. If black Americans do not, they are destined to remain as they have been for almost four centuries, the people with the least amount of power in America.

Historically, Black Americans Have Been An Uneducated, Unenlightened People

One of the justifications used by "civilized," Christian Americans for their enslavement of Africans was that they were saving Africans from a primitive existence on an uncivilized, unenlightened continent. In fact, long before 1619, the year the first blacks were brought to America, African societies had many established forms of government. Most African societies had agricultural based economies. Africans had many complex social institutions within their many intricate cultures and they expressed their sense of the aesthetic through their music, dance, and art.

In truth, the primitive, uncivilized, unenlightened existence of Africans began when they were taken off their continent, put into chains, packed into slave ships, and sent off to America. It is certain that these Africans did not believe that they were going to America to be civilized and enlightened. Indeed, so many Africans were being kidnapped during the height of the slave trade that it was rumored in Africa that white men were cannibals and were in fact eating their captives.

A second justification used by civilized, Christian Americans for the enslavement of Africans was that slavery was a part of the natural order of the universe. The proof, they claimed, was how willingly Africans submitted to Slavery and how well they adjusted to it. Of course, nothing could have been further from the truth.

Beyond the slave revolts, the Nat Turner revolt of 1831 being the largest and most notable, beyond the open acts of defiance in the face of cruel and inhumane punishment, there was a truth that was obvious to all but the most deluded proponents of Slavery. That truth was that blacks Americans hated Slavery and often took every opportunity short of subordination to register their displeasure. The truth was that, although America tried mightily for two and a half centuries, it could not break the spirit of blacks Americans or extinguish their desire and yearning for freedom.

How then did white America managed to keep millions of black Americans in Slavery for two hundred and forty-six years? How could they control so many people for such a long period of time with a minimum of short-lived, unsuccessful revolts? These may seem to be somewhat trite questions unless one has actually enslaved a people or have, at least, studied the process. The point is that it is not at all easy to subjugate and enslave a people. It is, in fact, an incredibly monumental endeavor.

White Americans developed their expertise in enslaving black Americans in much the same way that they developed their expertise in growing tobacco and cotton, destroying Native American societies, and making six-month journeys across the country in covered wagons. They began with on-the-job training on a small scale, developed a knowledge base, and disseminated that knowledge to current and future generations of white Americans.

White America also had the advantage of longevity. If Slavery had lasted only fifty or one hundred years, white America may not have become such experts in enslaving black Americans. However, with white Americans being in the enslavement business for two hundred and forty-six years, how could such a resourceful, industrious, knowledgeable people not develop a level of expertise that was unique in the history of humankind?

During two and half centuries of Slavery, white America learned and perfected various techniques and established a number of tenets for training and controlling black Americans. These were passed down from generation to generation by tradition and law. There were, however, underlying principles that every proponent of Slavery knew was necessary to perpetuate Slavery: "Keep slaves in fear and remove all vestiges of civilization and keep them ignorant."

Keep Slaves In Fear

According to writings of the Slavery era, the most successful way to train slaves was to begin by instilling the fear factor in them. Slaves were to be kept in constant awe of their master's enormous power. Slaves were to be continuously reminded of their personal inferiority. And slaves were to be constantly reminded of their helplessness in order to create a sense of dependency. However, because any white American could own slaves, and given the relative strengths and weaknesses to be found in human nature, white America did not leave it solely to slave owners to enforce the fear factor that was necessary to perpetuate Slavery. Every slave state had what was known as slave codes to ensure that the regulation and control of slaves met a minimum standard.

Fundamentally, all slave codes were similar. At the heart of every state's codes was the requirement that slaves submit to their masters and respect all whites. The Louisiana slave codes of 1806 states that "The condition of the slave being merely a passive one, his subordination to his master and to all who represent him is not susceptible of modification or restriction." The codes add that a slave "owes to his master, and to his family, a respect without bounds, and an absolute obedience, and he is consequently to execute all the orders which he receives from him, his said master, or from them."

A slave was to neither raise his hand against a white man, nor use insulting language. A look, a pointing of a finger, refusing or neglecting to step out of the way when a white person approached were all interpreted as insolence. "The power of the master must be absolute, to render the submission of the slave perfect," a southern judge once affirmed.   Short of deliberately killing or maliciously maiming a slave, a slave owner had absolute power over his property.

Make Them Ignorant And Keep Them Ignorant

Slaves codes also specifically addressed the other half of the equation for maintaining the enslavement of people who desperately wanted to be free.   White America realized that in order to keep slaves ignorant it had to control their movement and restrict their ability to communicate with others.

A slave was not to be "at large" without a pass, which he must show to any white man who asked to see it. Slaves were not to practice medicine or to administer medicine to whites.   "A slave under the pretence of practicing medicine," warned a Tennessee judge, "might convey intelligence from one plantation to another, and thus enable the slaves to act in concert."   A gathering of more than a few (usually five) slaves away from their master's premises was an "unlawful assembly" if unattended by a white person.   Farms and plantations employing slaves were to be under the supervision of resident white men and never left under the sole direction of slave foremen.

A system of slave patrols, often loosely connected with the state militia, existed in every slave state.   Their purpose was "to visit all negro quarters and other places suspected of having therein unlawful assemblies and to arrest such slaves as may stroll from one plantation to another without permission." A slave was legally a runaway if found without a pass beyond a certain prescribed distance from home: eight miles in Mississippi, twenty in Missouri, and so forth.

Many of these same types of restrictions also applied to black Americans who were not slaves. In many states, assembly was restricted and curfews imposed on free black Americans. In South Carolina and other states, black seamen were arrested and held in custody while their vessels were in port. Whenever the opportunity presented itself, free black Americans were moved out of slave states. And, in some slave states, if free black Americans left, they were prohibited by law from returning. Free black Americans could make contracts and own property but they were always at the mercy of white Americans who sought to deprive them of their property as well as their freedom. Black Americans were presumed to be slaves and the burden was on them to prove that they were free.

In addition to restricting the movement and assembly of slaves, slaves codes specifically addressed the need to keep slaves in a state of ignorance. A slave was not to preach except to his master's own slaves, on his master's premises, in the presence of whites. Slaves were not to beat drums or blow horns. No person, not even the slave's master, was to teach a slave to read or write, employ him in setting type in a printing office, or give him books or pamphlets. Heavy fines were imposed on white Americans who taught slaves to read or write.

In the minds of many white Americans, the greater sin was not the cold-blooded murder of a slave; it was teaching a slave or allowing a slave to think that he should be free or equal. Indeed, the reality is that some white Americans received harsher punishments for educating black Americans than other white Americans received for killing blacks Americans.

The Africans who were brought to America were civilized and, in their world, knowledgeable. However, the process of dehumanizing them began even before they arrived in America. They were then made to live a primitive life style while they toiled from dawn to dusk, day after day, year after year until premature old age or an early death freed them from their miserable existence.

Most slaves lived and died within a few miles of where they were born and raised. They never had the opportunity to see, and they did not have the knowledge to fully comprehend, the greatness of the nation they were building. White America could not have asked for a better result. Keeping black Americans in a state of ignorance was white America's most effective strategy for perpetuating Slavery for the two and a half centuries that it existed in America.

White America's strategy of keeping black Americans in a state of ignorance continued during the century of the Jim Crow era. The education of black Americans was one of America's lowest priorities. What education there was for black Americans was separate and substandard. Even today, there is a substantial difference in the amount of money spent to educate blacks Americans versus the amount spent to educate white Americans. It is, therefore, easy enough to argue that white America is attempting to keep the last vestige of Slavery alive by continuing to keep blacks Americans in a state of ignorance.

For three hundred and eighty years, the quality and the level of education attained by white Americans have, by law and tradition, exceeded the quality and the level of education attained by black Americans. Considering the obstacles they have had to overcome, black Americans can be proud that they are as close as they are to educational equivalency with white Americans. However, black America's task is far from complete.

Black America's struggle for absolute equality will never be won until black America's level of education equals or exceeds white America's. When that goal is reached, black America will have finally honored the memory of an unknown and uncelebrated group of black Americans who were beaten, mutilated, or killed. These black Americans were the slaves who had the courage to pick up a pen, a piece of paper, or a book in an attempt to find knowledge and enlightenment on the "Dark Continent" they knew as America.

Presently, Black Americans Are An Uneducated, Unenlightened People

During two hundred and forty-six years of Slavery, it was illegal to educate black Americans. During the one hundred and three years of the Jim Crow era, educating black Americans was one of America's lowest priorities. In the last thirty years, black America has not given a high enough priority to educating black Americans. The end results of these unfortunate circumstances are reflected in the following information and statistics.

Reading Proficiency
Rankings For High School Seniors: 1994

Rank	Racial Or Ethnic Group
1	White (Non-Hispanic)
2	Asian / Pacific Islander
3	American Indian / Alaskan Native
4	Hispanic
5	Black Americans

Mathematics Proficiency
Rankings For High School Seniors: 1994

Rank	Racial Or Ethnic Group
1	Asian / Pacific Islander
2	White (Non-Hispanic)
3	Hispanic
4	American Indian / Alaskan Native
5	Black Americans

Science Proficiency
Rankings For High School Seniors: 1994

Rank	Racial Or Ethnic Group
1	Asian / Pacific Islander
2	White (Non-Hispanic)
3	American Indian / Alaskan Native
4	Hispanic
5	Black Americans

Completion Of 4 Years Of High School Or More
Americans 25 Years Old And Older

(Percentages)

Year	All Races	White	Black
1940	24.5	26.1	7.7
1947	33.1	35.0	13.6
1957	41.6	43.2	18.4
1965	49.0	51.3	27.2
1970	55.2	57.4	33.7
1975	62.5	64.5	42.5
1980	68.6	70.5	51.2
1985	73.9	75.5	59.8
1990	77.6	79.1	66.2
1996	81.7	82.8	74.3

Completion Of 4 Years Of College Or More
Americans 25 Years Old And Older

(Percentages)

Year	All Races	White	Black
1940	4.6	4.9	1.3
1947	5.4	5.7	2.5
1957	7.6	8.0	2.9
1965	9.4	9.9	4.7
1970	11.0	11.6	4.5
1975	13.9	14.5	6.4
1980	17.0	17.8	7.9
1985	19.4	20.0	11.1
1990	21.3	22.0	11.3
1996	23.6	24.3	13.6

College Degrees Earned
Percentage Earned By Black Americans

Level Of Degree	Total Degrees Awarded In 1981	% Earned By Blacks In 1981	Total Degrees Awarded In 1993	% Earned By Blacks In 1993
Associate	410,174	8.6%	508,154	8.3%
Bachelor	934,800	6.5%	1,159,931	6.7%
Master	294,183	5.8%	368,701	5.4%
Doctor	32,839	3.9%	42,021	3.2%

There is a great deal that could be said regarding the above and other such data. Hundreds or even thousands of suppositions, hypotheses, and theories are possible. There are, however, some obvious conclusions that can be agreed upon regarding education in America and, specifically, the education of black Americans.

- The 1940's were a pivotal point in time in the way formal education was regarded in America. In 1940, one hundred and sixty-four years after the signing of the Declaration of Independence, less than twenty-five percent of American adults had graduated from high school. Within twenty-five years, the percentage had doubled. By 1996, another thirty-one years later, more that eight of every ten American adults had graduated from high school.

- The 1940's were also a pivotal period for black America with regard to formal education. In 1940, less than eight of every one hundred black Americans had graduated from high school. Within twenty-five years, the percentage of black graduates had almost quadrupled. By 1996, nearly seventy-five of every one hundred black Americans had completed at least four years of high school.

- In 1940, only four out of every three hundred black Americans graduated from college. By the 1960's, more than four out of every one hundred black Americans were earning college degrees. A case can be made that the surge in black high school graduates and the increase of college educated black Americans helped to ignite and sustain the Civil Rights movement. Most of the leaders of the movement were well educated and many, like Martin Luther King, Jr., had earned doctor's degrees. It can also be argued that the tripling of black high school and college graduates since 1960 has helped to fuel black America's struggle for socioeconomic equality.

- America has become a nation where a formal education of at least four years of high school is routinely expected and "universally" accomplished. In a nation where diversity is the rule, there are very few things that are as universal as formal education. Less than eighty-two percent of Americans have ever voted, less than eighty-two percent attend church on a regular basis, and less than eighty-two percent eat hot dogs or even mom's apple pie.

- Because formal education is now so universal, it is impossible for formal education, or lack of formal education, to not have an impact on the economic status of Americans. Even if there were a reason to hire Americans with little or no formal education, it could be difficult to find them. A prospective employer advertising that a high school education was not a requirement would still, almost certainly, end up with more candidates who had completed high school than candidates who had not.

- It is impossible for black America's shortfall in formal education to not contribute to its lower economic status. For example: a company advertises that it has thousands of job openings paying twice the minimum wage but fails to mention that high school graduation is a requirement. For every one hundred white Americans who apply for the jobs, seventeen would not be qualified. For every one hundred black Americans who apply for the jobs, twenty-six would not be qualified. If the same company were hiring all recent college graduates at fifty thousand dollars a year, twenty-four white Americans would be hired for every fourteen black Americans.

- Black America's lower economic status contributes to many of its social problems. Educated, gainfully employed Americans have no need for welfare and their children are more likely to live in two parent households. College educated Americans rarely engage in felonious criminal activities and are also less likely to be victims of crime. Economically successful Americans are less likely to abuse hard drugs and to engage in other risky behavior.

- Black America has made a great deal more progress in reducing the gap in secondary education than in reducing the gap in higher education. In terms of high school education, in 1940 only thirty percent of black Americans were as educated as white Americans. By 1996, this percentage had risen to ninety percent. In terms of college education, in 1940 twenty-seven percent of black Americans were as educated as white Americans. Unfortunately, by 1996, this percentage had risen to only fifty-six percent.

- The gap that exists between education attained by white Americans and by black Americans widens based on the level of education attained. The smallest gap is in the completion of primary school. The gap widens for black and white high school graduates. It is even wider for undergraduate degrees earned and wider yet for postgraduate degrees earned. In some areas, white Americans, based on their percentage of population, earn up to ten times more graduate, technical, and doctoral degrees than black Americans do.

- In light of two and a half centuries of Slavery followed by a century of the Jim Crow era, it is to black America's credit that its educational level is as close as it is to the educational level of white America. However, while black America has made significant progress, it still lags significantly behind white America. Black Americans must understand that, in America today and in America in the future, the most economically successful Americans are and will continue to be the Americans with the most formal education.

If, in fact, the ultimate solution to black America's socioeconomic problems is for more black Americans to attain more education and better education, why are most black Americans not aware of or convinced of this fact?

Why is the quest for educational equality not the number one priority of black America? Why, in fact, is formal education not one of black America's obsessions?

One response to these questions is that black Americans do not receive a quality primary and secondary education and this limits their ability to attain higher education. Another response is that college is expensive and black Americans are so economically disadvantaged that they must enter the workforce as quickly as possible. Perhaps the answer is that black Americans have been conditioned to have little or no appreciation for or love of knowledge. Maybe some black Americans simply do not understand the power of knowledge.

In the past, white America chose to and had the power to keep black Americans uneducated and unenlightened. Today, if education is not the number one priority of black America, it is because black America does not choose to use its power and resources to educate and enlighten black Americans. And, for this failing, black Americans have only themselves to blame.

Knowledge, As A Product Of Education, Is The Only Salvation For Black America

"Black Americans were one of the most abused, most oppressed, and most long-suffering minorities in the history of humankind."

This is the legacy of black America for the first three hundred and eighty years of its existence. If black America is to ever have a different legacy, black Americans must accept that knowledge, as a product of education, is black America's only salvation.

Some black Americans will fervently agree that the only salvation for black America is the successful completion of the goals and objectives of Project 2019. They will argue that only Project 2019 can, in one generation, elevate black America from its underclass status. They will understand that if Project 2019 succeeds, black America will be propelled into the mainstream of American society.

Other black Americans will agree that Project 2019 is a worthwhile endeavor. However, they will not be convinced that its objectives can or will ever be accomplished. But they will agree that any progress that can be made in increasing the number of black

Americans who earn college degrees would be beneficial to black America.

Still, other black Americans will have doubts regarding the impact Project 2019 would have on black America even if its objectives were accomplished. They will, however, concede that elevating the educational level of black America is one component of the process that is required to improve the socioeconomic status of black America.

There may never be a consensus on the best way to accomplish Project 2019, a consensus on whether Project 2019 can in fact be accomplished, or a consensus on the impact that Project 2019 would have even if it were successful. However, the good news is that, regardless of the position taken regarding Project 2019, at least ninety percent of black Americans will agree that it would be beneficial to elevate the educational level of black America. This is good news because the first and most important step in accomplishing the objectives of Project 2019 is for black Americans to believe that education is a worthwhile goal.

Almost all black Americans are in agreement that elevating the educational level of black America would be beneficial to black Americans. This is an important consideration when responding to two of the most crucial issues that black America must eventually resolve. "Can education and knowledge save black America?" "Is education and knowledge the only way to save black America?"

Can Formal Education Save Black America?

There is no way to prove statistically to everyone's or anyone's satisfaction that education can save black America from another one hundred years of being relegated to the lowest socioeconomic level in America. Before the data could be gathered and the number crunching begun, questions would be raised, debate would ensue, and disagreements would be voiced regarding the validity of the data, the process, and the methodology to be used to prove the case. However, a complicated study may not be necessary if simple logic will do.

What would be the ramifications of black America having, based on its percentage of population, twice as many black attorneys as white attorneys, twice as many black physicians as white physicians, and twice as many black engineers as white engineers? What if there were twice as many black architects as white architects, twice as many black accountants as white accountants, and twice as many black bankers as white bankers? The result of this scenario would be that black America would not occupy the lowest socioeconomic standing in America.

If the above scenario seems familiar, it is because it is approximately the current situation in America. Of course, the difference is that white America, based on its percentage of population, has several times more attorneys, physicians, engineers, architects, accountants, and bankers. Not only do these professionals personally contribute to the socioeconomic status of white America, they also have the power to contribute by making jobs available, awarding contracts, lending money, and so forth to other white Americans. They also have the means to send their children to the best schools, thereby maintaining their educational superiority.

Of course, it may be argued that a higher educational level is not the only reason why white America enjoys a high socioeconomic standing. However, at this point in America's history, it is the ultimate reason. Doctors are doctors and lawyers are lawyers because of education, not because of race. A black American with a medical degree can become a doctor; a white high school dropout can not. A white American with a law degree can become a lawyer; a black high school dropout can not.

There are factors other than education that contribute to the ability of people to rise to, and remain on, a higher socioeconomic level: family connections, nepotism, college legacies, good credit, reserve capital, access to risk capital, and so forth. Unfortunately for black America, many of these factors are the benefits that come with a higher socioeconomic status. In a sense, it is a catch-22. It is akin to not being able to get a particular job without experience and not being able to get experience without the job. Of course, this can not always be true or no one would ever get the job. What is true is that black Americans will just have to work harder and work smarter to obtain the advantages currently enjoyed by white Americans.

Is Formal Education The "Only" Salvation?

The final question to be answered is whether education is the "only" way to save black America from another one hundred years of being relegated to the lowest socioeconomic level in America. For the proponents of Project 2019, the answer is "yes" and Project 2019 is the only way to this salvation.

Project 2019 is the only program, project, or strategy that addresses all the worse problems of black America at their core. Project 2019 is the only program, project, or strategy with concise, reasonable goals. Project 2019 is the only program, project, or strategy that has a measurable, attainable objective with a specific, achievable time frame. Project 2019 is the only program, project, or strategy that assigns the task of saving black America exclusively to black Americans, the only people who can save black America. And, finally, Project 2019 is the only program, project, or strategy that, when successfully completed, will inaugurate the beginning of a new, more positive legacy for black America.

Is Project 2019 the only way to save black America? Until someone can demonstrate to the proponents of Project 2019 a better program, project, or strategy to save black America, then the answer will be "yes."

Black America Must Realize The Urgency Of The Mission

Black Americans have faced three monumental challenges in the three hundred and eighty years they have been in America. The first challenge was to end Slavery. That challenge was met in 1865. The second challenge was to secure civil rights for all black Americans. This challenge was successfully concluded as of 1968. Black America's third and final challenge is to attain socioeconomic equality with white America. Socioeconomic equality is as crucial to the ultimate success of black America as was ending Slavery and obtaining civil rights. Black Americans will never be truly equal in America until this challenge is met.

In order for black Americans to attain socioeconomic equality, there must be a change in the conditions and the circumstances that currently exist in America. This change will come about as a result of "evolution" or it will be the result of "revolution." Evolutionary change is a slow, methodical, subdued mode of change. With a few nudges or an occasional push, a change can be directed and accomplished over an extended period of time. Revolutionary change is, of course, much more dynamic. It is characterized by events and actions and many wide-ranging activities that are all designed to affect the change. The end results are that the change occurs in a much shorter time span.

In fact, for most social changes, there is an evolutionary component and a revolutionary component. In the case of Slavery, the evolutionary component lasted for more than two centuries. Over that time, more and more Americans, along with the rest of the world, decided that slavery in general and American Slavery in particular was wrong. The revolutionary component of the ending of Slavery was the Civil War. In the case of black Americans obtaining civil rights, the evolutionary component lasted almost a century. The revolutionary component was the Civil Rights movement of the 1960's.

There are no rules that dictate the length of either the evolutionary or revolutionary component of change. However, given that a change will eventually occur as a result of evolution, the longer the evolutionary process, the easier the revolution. And, of course, if the evolution process lasts long enough, there is no need for a revolution. On the other hand, the earlier in the evolutionary process a revolution occurs, the more difficult it is for the revolution to succeed.

This is to say that, even without the Civil War, Slavery would have eventually ended. It may have taken another fifty or one hundred years, but the evolutionary direction of humankind dictated the inevitable end of Slavery. This is also to say that black Americans could have ended Slavery one hundred years earlier had it been possible for them to create a revolution and if they had been willing to sacrifices hundreds of thousands or even millions of black lives.

This is also the case for black America's struggle to obtain civil rights. If the Civil Rights movement had never occurred, in fifty or one hundred years, black Americans would have evolved into being fully franchised citizens of the United States. Again, black Americans could have obtained civil rights decades earlier if they had been able and willing to mount a revolution. But, again, there would have been a tremendous price to be paid in terms of pain and suffering and lives lost.

If black America continues down the evolutionary path that it is now on, in fifty or one hundred years, black America will most likely reach socioeconomic equality with white America. On the other hand, if a revolutionary component, specifically, Project 2019, is introduced into this struggle, this time frame will be reduced considerably.

Unlike the revolutionary components of the struggle to end Slavery and the struggle to obtain civil rights, a revolution to reach socioeconomic equality could be won without the cost of any lives. That is the good news. The bad news is that, although the struggle for socioeconomic equality may not be as dangerous, the enemies of this struggle are in many ways more formidable than racist white America. These enemies include ignorance and apathy and they exist within black America.

Introducing a revolutionary component into the struggle for socioeconomic equality will lessen the amount of time it will take to win the struggle. This should be reason and motivation enough to do so. However, there are in fact other reasons why black America must recognize and respond to the urgency of this mission.

The Mission Will Not Get Any Easier

As America enters the twenty-first century, it continues to evolve and black America must evolve with it. At the beginning of the twentieth century, less than twelve of every one hundred Americans earned even a high school diploma. At the end of the twentieth century, twenty-four of every one hundred Americans earn a college degree. At the beginning of the twentieth century, it was enough to just be able to read, to write, and to do simple math. In the twenty-first century, the equivalent of a college degree may be required for all jobs that pay more than subsistence wages.

Too many black Americans do not understand what a service-based economy is, what the benefits of a global economy are, or what NAFTA really means to them. What it all mean is that black America is already much too far behind. Every day that black Americans do not make any progress, it becomes that much more difficult for them to catch up. One problem is that attaining knowledge is a cumulative process. It is impossible to understand algebra without first knowing how to add and subtract. Another problem is that white America is not standing still waiting for black America to catch up. And it would be naïve to think that white America would not accelerate its pace when black America begins to close the education and knowledge gap.

The 13th Amendment to the Constitution made all American citizens "equally free." Civil rights laws gave all American citizens "equal rights." However, there will never be a law in America mandating socioeconomic equality. Only black Americans can ensure that they are "equally educated" and "equally knowledgeable" and therefore in a position to attain socioeconomic equality.

It Could Already Be Too Little, Too Late

In one respect, ending Slavery and obtaining civil rights were not very complicated. The only requirements were a consensus of the American people and the addition of a few new laws. Indeed, it is entirely within the realm of possibilities that both could have been accomplished without bloodshed or loss of lives. There was, of course, resistance to these changes and it resulted in the Civil War and the Civil Rights movement. However, beyond this resistance, there was never any doubt that Slavery could be ended and that civil rights could be given to black Americans.

On the other hand, all Americans, black and white, could agree today that there should be socioeconomic equality for all black Americans and it would have absolutely no effect on the socioeconomic status of black

America. Indeed, new laws could be passed, new programs initiated, and billions of dollars pumped into black communities and this still would not guarantee that black America would reach socioeconomic equality with white America.

One problem is the scope and the magnitude of the mission. Another problem is that, in the history of humankind, there are few, if any, appropriate models on which to pattern such an endeavor. There is no guarantee that the first truly serious effort will succeed. Several approaches over many decades may be required before a solution is found. And there is also the possibility that black Americans will forever remain an underclass in American society. Clearly, these considerations should speak volumes to black Americans regarding the urgency of the mission.

There May Never Be A Better Time

Another reason for urgency is to capitalize on the prevailing sense of fairness and justice that currently exists in America. Open, hostile, illegal racism is now less acceptable than it has been at any time since the arrival of blacks in America. Although America is still far from being a color-blind society, it is as fair and open a society as it has been in four centuries. Black Americans must act now while the mood and the circumstances of the country are conducive to change.

Under ordinary circumstances, it is not likely that race relations would take a huge step backward. However, extraordinary things do happen. If America were to suffer huge losses as a result of a disastrous war, a devastating terrorist attack, or a 1929 type depression, the people in the lowest socioeconomic classes would ultimately be the ones who would suffer the most. If such a catastrophe were to occur, it would be difficult, if not impossible, for black America to recover.

In addition to pragmatic reasons why black Americans should have a sense of urgency about reaching socioeconomic equality, there are other very good reasons. There is the opportunity to demonstrate to America and the world the resilience, the unity, and the greatness of black America. There is the debt that is owed to the millions of black Americans who lived, suffered, and died to bring the current generation of black Americans to this point in their history. However, one of the best reasons why black Americans should have a sense of urgency about their mission of socioeconomic equality is because of what was once called "black pride."

Every black American alive today has the unique opportunity to make a historic contribution to black America that their grandchildren or great-grandchildren can look back on with pride. In fact, since most black Americans who are alive today will be alive in the year 2019, their children, their grandchildren, or their great-grandchildren can personally tell them how proud they are of what they accomplished.

Socioeconomic Equality:
By Any Means Necessary

There is no detailed plan for the introduction and implementation of Project 2019 and its mission, to elevate the socioeconomic status of black America. Nor is there a formal five, ten, or twenty-year plan to sustain and successfully execute Project 2019. Similar to other movements, including the Civil Rights movement, the struggle for socioeconomic equality must be managed, in many ways, as a work in progress.

There are other similarities between the two movements. Like the Civil Rights movement, there is only one way to initiate Project 2019: by any means necessary. There is only one way to sustain Project 2019: by any means necessary. There is only one way to bring Project 2019 to a successful conclusion: by any means necessary.

The expression, "by any means necessary," has a different connotation to those who are participating in a struggle than it does to those who are not participating in the struggle. Those who fight the battle are resolute and sincere in their belief that they are doing the right things for the right reasons. And they steadfastly believe that they must win at all costs. For those who are on the other

185

side of the struggle, the expression, "by any means necessary," conjures up images of extremists or fanatics intent on accomplishing something that they do not agree with and in many cases do not even understand.

This scenario certainly fits the Civil Rights movement. In his lifetime, Martin Luther King was considered a "troublemaker" and was genuinely disliked by a very large percentage of white Americans. Malcolm X was distrusted and hated by most white Americans during his lifetime. Today, Malcolm X is honored on a United States postal stamp.

But, unlike the Civil Rights movement, the struggle for socioeconomic equality is not at its core a black versus white struggle. The struggle for socioeconomic equality is a black movement, by blacks Americans, for the betterment of black America. Indeed, the struggle will take place almost exclusively in black communities.

Is it, therefore, necessary to adopt such an extreme position as "accomplishing black America's goal of socioeconomic equality by any means necessary?" Without any doubt, the answer is yes. The enemy in the struggle for socioeconomic equality is a different enemy than the enemy in the struggle for civil rights. However, this new enemy is also defined and characterized by ignorance and apathy. And when combating such formidable forces, an extreme offense offers the only chance for victory.

During the Civil Rights movement, "by any means necessary" meant having the courage to face club wielding state troopers and vicious police dogs. In the struggle for socioeconomic equality it will mean having the courage to go to street corners and demand that gang members leave black children alone so they can pursue their education. During the Civil Rights movement, "by any means necessary" meant making a commitment to sit for hours at segregated lunch counters and face the abuse of hostile white workers and angry white patrons. In the struggle for socioeconomic equality it will mean making a commitment to sit down every day with black children and spend time studying, reading, and discussing the benefits of knowledge and education.

During the Civil Rights movement, "by any means necessary" meant having enough black pride and black unity to march on Washington and to march down the hate-filled streets of other major American cities. In the struggle for socioeconomic equality it will mean having enough black pride and black unity to support black businesses, black business cooperatives, and black colleges. During the Civil Rights movement, for many people, "by any means necessary" meant that they were willing to sacrifice their personal freedom or even their lives for the cause. In the struggle for socioeconomic equality, for some people, it will also mean that they are willing to sacrifice their personal freedom or even their lives for the cause.

Although the expression, "by any means necessary," may sound ominous and have negative connotations for those who are not a part of the struggle, for the most part, it is all about personal sacrifices for those who are a part of the struggle. This is certainly the case in black America's struggle for socioeconomic equality. There are sacrifices that black Americans must make if they are to succeed. One sacrifice that all black Americans can make begins with them coming to terms with the fact that the current generation of adult black Americans can not be saved.

Black America's socioeconomic standing will be the lowest in America in the year 2000, in the year 2005, and in the year 2010. The best efforts of black America can not change this fact. Even the best efforts of black America in conjunction with the best efforts of white America can not change this fact. Short of some sort of divine intervention, there is little that can or will be done over the next five or ten years that will result in black America reaching socioeconomic equality with white America. The statistics and the facts speak clearly for themselves.

The harsh reality is that there is little or no socioeconomic salvation for the overwhelming majority of black Americans who are over the age of eighteen, who are poor, and who are poorly educated. They will not be doctors. They will not be lawyers. They will not be successful businessmen and women. The majority of black Americans who are over the age of eighteen, who are poor, and who are poorly educated are destined to live lives of economic deprivation. They will live from paycheck to paycheck, they will struggle to make ends meet, and many will survive off of unemployment and welfare when they can not find low paying jobs requiring unskilled labor.

While this may be a harsh reality to face, an even harsher reality is that this generation of black Americans is the nineteenth lost generation of black Americans. And there is a harsher reality yet. Unless black America starts looking forward rather than bemoaning the past and complaining about the present, the next generation will be the twentieth lost generation of black Americans.

It should not come as a surprise that fifteen to twenty-five years of concerted effort is required to elevate black America to socioeconomic equality. Nor should it come as a surprise that the current generation of black Americans, those who must make the sacrifices, will not be the main beneficiaries of this effort. All black Americans must accept this fact and direct their attention and efforts to black children. They are the future. They are the hope of black America. There is a question that all black Americans must unselfishly and continuously ask themselves regarding everything they do or anything that is done for them. "Will this help to make my life better, or will this enable the next generation of black Americans to successfully compete with the rest of America in the year 2019?"

Of course, a movement is not only about work, pain, and sacrifice. A movement also has many positive elements such as hope, faith, motivation, inspiration, love, and joy. "By any means necessary" could also mean incorporating the specific goals and objectives of Project 2019 into Kwanzaa celebrations. Project 2019 back-to-school parades could be held on American streets named after Martin Luther King to reinforce the spirit of the movement. February, Black History Month, could be a time to review, to measure progress, to reflect on accomplishments of Project 2019, and to set new annual goals and objectives.

There will eventually be plans and strategies for accomplishing Project 2019. However, none of the specific step by step details will be important until the first and most crucial step is taken to reach educational equality. The first step is not to ask how it will be done. The first step is for black America to resolve that it will be done. If it is resolved that it will be done, then the specific means by which it will be accomplished will begin to flow. If black America resolves that it will be done, it will be done: by any means necessary.

The Enemies Of
Project 2019

The mission of Project 2019 is to elevate the socioeconomic status of black America. Because this is an instance of blacks Americans working for the betterment of black America, one might conclude that the only enemies of Project 2019 would be avowed racists and other extremists. Unfortunately, this is not the case.

History teaches that it is impossible to affect social change without reactions from those who are not in one hundred percent agreement with the change. These reactions can range from curious concern to intractable opposition. Possible areas of concern or dissension include the reason for the change, the timing of the change, the nature of the change, the scope of the change, and one's role, or lack of a role, in the change.

It is important for black America to anticipate all conceivable opposition to Project 2019. It is especially important for proponents of Project 2019 to understand that most of the opposition to Project 2019 will come from within black America. Proponents of Project 2019 must remember that it is always a costly and often a fatal mistake to not know one's enemies or to not be prepared to deal with them.

The Skeptics And The Doubters

Some of the first enemies of Project 2019 to surface will be "skeptics and doubters." They will question the value of Project 2019. They may argue that racism is still the biggest problem in America today and produce statistics to show that black high school and college graduates earn less money than white Americans with the same amount of education.

The "skeptics and doubters" will not accept that the ultimate solution is for more black Americans to own more companies and for more black Americans to occupy upper management positions in corporate America. They will not believe that this is the best way, and perhaps the only way, to ensure that black Americans receive fair and equitable treatment in the work force.

Those Without Faith

The "faithless" will also be enemies of Project 2019. They will be represented by black Americans who are downtrodden and by those who have seen or experienced the worse effects of racism. They may remind black America how the 14th and 15th Amendments to the Constitution failed to solve black America's problems. They may point out how the Civil Rights movement and Affirmative Action did not end black America's three and a half centuries of pain and suffering.

Those without faith will be sure that, in the end, Project 2019 will not change the fate of black America.

They will not be able to see the progress that black America has made. Nor will they understand that much of this progress can be attributed to their ancestors having never lost their faith.

The Impatient And The Demanding

Enemies of Project 2019 will include the "impatient" and the "demanding." They will discover that the value of Project 2019 will be realized over a period of years and that Project 2019 is of no immediate personal benefit to them. They will insist that there must be a better way. They will complain that twenty years is too long to wait for something that will ultimately not benefit them.

The "impatient" and the "demanding" will not understand that there is no immediate solution for a problem that has festered for hundreds of years. They will not care that it will take the selflessness of one generation of black Americans to create a better America for all future generations of black Americans.

The Selfish And The Miserly

A cruel combination of enemies of Project 2019 will be the "selfish" and the "miserly." They will be represented by black Americans who have "made it" and who see the struggle only through their own experiences. They may declare that if they could do it, then those "lazy blacks still in the ghetto" can do it. They will see the struggle as an individual endeavor and conclude that it was hard enough to get "theirs," hard enough to keep what they have, and it is not their responsibility to save the rest of black America.

The "selfish" and the "miserly" do not know or have forgotten that thousands died in order for them to have an opportunity to get "theirs." They also do not know or have forgotten that they are black Americans and black Americans are the least powerful people in America. The "selfish" and the "miserly" must understand that they are in the position that free blacks were in during Slavery. Until all black Americans are "free and equal," then freedom and equality is not guaranteed to any black American.

The Prideful

Some of the most tragic enemies of Project 2019 will be the "prideful." They will not be able to accept the merits of Project 2019 because Project 2019 does not perfectly match their vision for solving black America's socioeconomic problems. They will see Project 2019 as being in competition with their philosophies and will not believe that any differences can be resolved. This is unfortunate because they have given the most thought to the problem and have searched the hardest for a solution. They are the ones that Project 2019 needs most because they are the ones most qualified to lead the struggle.

Racists And Extremists

A predictable enemy of Project 2019 will be "white racists." They will make every effort to discredit and derail Project 2019. The tactics of white racists are well known, their motives are clearly understood, and their power to negatively impact Project 2019 will be limited.

On the other hand, a not so predictable but much more unsettling enemy of Project 2019 will be "black racists." For various reasons, some of which will be heartfelt and sincere, they will see Project 2019 as a betrayal to black America. They may argue that attempting to "beat the white man at his own game" is a waste of effort. They may insist that the black man has a higher calling or a more spiritual purpose. Black racists will not see themselves as racists and will not understand that they are just as misguided as white racists.

The Apathetic

Second only to ignorance, the most formidable enemy of Project 2019 will be apathy. The "apathetic" will be formidable because their numbers will make them the largest group of enemies. They will also be formidable because they will be the most difficult to recognize.

When confronted, they may pay lip service to the merits of reaching socioeconomic equality through formal education and they may indicate that they support Project 2019. However, when there is no one around, they will do little or nothing to further the cause. And when called upon to do their part, the apathetic will always have something more important to do. The apathetic will not understand that if they are not a part of the solution, then they are a part of the problem.

The Uninformed And The Unenlightened

Without any doubt, the most insidious, pervasive, and formidable enemy of Project 2019 will be "ignorance." There is the initial level of ignorance that must be fought in order to get the message of Project 2019 to black America. There is a level of ignorance that must be overcome to convince black America of the merits and the possibilities of Project 2019. When this is successfully accomplished, there is, of course, the main challenge of Project 2019, eliminating ignorance in black America and replacing it with knowledge and enlightenment. And, while attempting to accomplish all of these things, the proponents of Project 2019 must deal with opposition to the movement that will be largely based on or fueled by ignorance.

There is, however, good news for the proponents of Project 2019. The enemies of Project 2019 are all, on some level, defined by ignorance. Ignorance is inherently a weakness. Additionally, the proponents of Project 2019 are operating from a position of strength. They have knowledge and enlightenment on their side and knowledge is power. Historically, knowledge and enlightenment have always defeated ignorance and fear. Ultimately, knowledge and enlightenment will prevail over the enemies of Project 2019.

The Heroes Of Project 2019

What did black America accomplish during the twenty-year period from 1959 to 1979? There is an easy answer to this question. Black America initiated, fought, and won a revolution to obtain and secure civil rights for black Americans. What did black America accomplish from 1979 to 1999? There is also an easy answer to this question. Compared to the previous twenty-year period, black America accomplished little or nothing and in some areas barely maintained the status quo.

In the year 2019, our children and grandchildren may well ask a similar question. What did black America accomplish during the first two decades of the twenty-first century? If black America accomplishes "little or nothing" from 1999 to 2019, then black Americans can write off most of the twenty-first century. If this is the case, black America should be prepared to continue its role as the base upon which white America builds its success and prosperity.

If the objectives and goals of Project 2019 are met, our children and grandchildren will have a number of accomplishments to list in response to the question. The most important accomplishment will be that blacks, for the first time since they arrived in America, will be as educated, as knowledgeable, and as enlightened as white Americans. After four hundred years in America, our children's and grandchildren's generation will be the first black generation truly prepared to compete with the rest of America on a level playing field.

While our children and grandchildren may believe they have their parents' generation to thank for their success, they should understand they owe equal amounts of gratitude to every past generation of black Americans. The current generation of black Americans would not have been in a position to make the final push to total equality if it had not been for the strength and wisdom of their parents, grandparents, and great-grandparents. And, of course, all black Americans owe a debt of gratitude to their ancestors who suffered the horrors and indignities of Slavery without ever giving up their dream of freedom – if not for themselves, then at least for their descendants. If, however, in the coming decades, our children and grandchildren wish to acknowledge the heroes of Project 2019, it is easy enough to anticipate who the heroes will be.

The Black Media

The black media can be heroes of Project 2019. The size of the black media is small when compared to the percentage of the black population. However, the overall impact of the black media on black America is enormous. Prior to the emergence of broadcast media and

198

Americans' modern life style, the black print media was unchallenged. And although black Americans currently own just over two percent of all television stations, in the future this percentage will increase and with it the impact of black television. The percentage of radio stations owned by black Americans is less than two percent. However, without question, black radio is today the black medium with the greatest impact on black America.

Although the number of black radio stations is small, nearly the same percentage of black Americans listens to these fewer black stations as the percentage of white Americans who listen to the more numerous white stations. By comparison, the black print media offers much less competition to the white print media and black television, at this point, can not compete with white television.

Black radio reaches the vast majority of black Americans, either directly or indirectly, on an almost daily basis. It has the capability to introduce and sustain Project 2019 more so than any other mass communication tool available to the black community. In addition to Project 2019 promotions and contests, black radio can help to ensure the success of Project 2019 by continuously reminding black America of the name, the purpose, and the progress of Project 2019.

Black Churches

Black churches can be heroes of Project 2019. In fact, many churches already have education departments or programs that are intended to encourage or assist in the education of their children. They, therefore, need only to incorporate the spirit and the unity of Project 2019 into their exiting programs. Other positive steps that can be taken include establishing or expanding scholarship funds and establishing or expanding tutoring programs. There are those who argue that more religion should be allowed into American schools. It is certainly just as appropriate to put more education into our churches.

For those black churches that do not emphasize the education of their children, they must begin doing so. During the Slavery era, an argument was made that a slave should be allowed to learn to read so that he might read the Bible. It was decided that the possibility of the slave losing his soul was not worth the risk that he might read something that would make him unhappy with his station in life. Today, any church not actively supporting the education of its children is guilty of equally misguided thinking.

Educational salvation must be only a small step below spiritual salvation in importance to black churches. Although God may wink at ignorance, there is no evidence that God approves of it. Additionally, there should be little doubt that it is easier to save the soul of a wise man than it is to save the soul of a fool. By embracing the benefits of education, black churches can be counted, as they should be, among the heroes of Project 2019.

Black Entertainers And Athletes

Black entertainers and professional athletes can and should be heroes of Project 2019 because, whether they like it or not, they are role models for young black Americans. The definition of "role model" is "a person whose behavior in a particular role is imitated by others." Note that it is not the role model who chooses to be or chooses not to be imitated by others. It is the "others" who, for better or worse, choose the role models and, more importantly, choose which roles to imitate. This is the reason parents can not raise their children by simply telling them to "do as I say, not as I do." It is also the reason entertainers and sports celebrities can not simply say "buy my music or the products that I endorse but ignore the fact that I abuse my family or do drugs."

Of course, everyone has options. If you want to avoid being a role model, then do not have children. You should also attempt to live a very quiet, very private life. This will lessen the possibility of others imitating your behavior. But, whatever you do, do not become a well-known entertainer or a star athlete. As an unavoidable consequence of your success and fame, there will children who will choose to imitate your behavior, behavior that may or may not have anything to do with your art or sport. Black artist and athletes must realize that they are not being paid to just sing, act, or shoot a basketball. They are being paid to make little boys and girls think they want to "be like Mike" and to convince their parents to buy them a CD or a particular brand of gym shoes.

Black professional athletes can also become heroes of Project 2019 by explaining to black children the realities of professional sports. They can testify that the road to becoming a superstar athlete is littered with the bodies and the dreams of hundreds of thousands of young black Americans who were competing for jobs that number only in the hundreds. They can explain to them that the odds of becoming a success in America are thousands of times greater if they spend two hours a day reading and studying than if they spend two hours a day playing basketball.

Black recording and performing artists and others in the entertainment field can use their celebrity status to promote and support Project 2019. More importantly, they can use the power of their art to further the cause of Project 2019. Considering the interest that could be generated by the subject matter as well as the nobility of the cause, it should not be a difficult challenge to create and produce interesting and exciting movies, plays, and songs with educating black Americans as a major theme.

Black Professionals

Black professionals can be heroes of Project 2019 by providing the business and technical expertise that will be required to make Project 2019 a success. The knowledge and the skills of black professionals, from teachers to judges and from politicians to publishers, will be essential in every phase of the movement. The expertise of black professionals can also be provided directly to young black Americans in the form of tutoring and mentoring. If every black architect, accountant, attorney, banker, doctor, engineer, and so forth were to tutor and mentor just one black child, it would go a long way towards making Project 2019 a success.

Black professionals, more so than any other segment of the black population, must step forward and support Project 2019. They have taken the path that Project 2019 declares to be the best path, the path that will lead to solutions for many of black America's problems. These black men and women have taken the path of formal education and they have succeeded as a result of it.

Based on all standard economic measurements and social indicators, black professionals are by far the most successful segment of the black population. Their lives are obvious and irrefutable proof that "the system works." Their success is one of the best arguments that can be made for what Project 2019 contends to be true; knowledge is power and knowledge, as a product of formal education, can save black America.

Black Families

Black families must be heroes of Project 2019. Indeed, the contributions of other heroes of Project 2019 will be severely limited without the support of black families. Family has always been the backbone of human civilization and it remains so today. Black families must certainly be the backbone of Project 2019 because the family unit is where children get their values, develop their character, and where they look to for various forms of support. Even more importantly, the family unit is where children begin their education and develop long lasting attitudes regarding education.

Education must start early for every black child. Black parents should begin reading to their children while they are still in the womb and they should read to them when they are infants and toddlers. All black families should establish a daily "home study period." There should be a consistent time in the evening when the television is turned off and the entire family spends time together on academic pursuits, above and beyond a student's daily homework. It has been said that, "a family that prays together, stays together." It can also be said that, "a family that learns together, succeeds together."

The importance of education must be stressed in every black family. "You must get a good education if you want to be successful" is a message that can be heard in many black American homes. This should be a mantra in the home of every black child in America. "You must get a good education if you want to be successful." It should be repeated morning, noon, and night and parents should take every possible opportunity to convince their children that it is a fact.

Parents must take an active interest in their children's homework, test grades, and final grades. They should insist on excellence and not allow their children to settle for mediocrity. For parents who truly love their children and want them to have a better life, there is no better way to demonstrate this than to insist on straight "A's" from kindergarten through college.

All Black Americans

Finally, each and every black American has the potential and the opportunity to be a hero of Project 2019. The oldest, the youngest, and everyone in between has a role to play. The most educated and the least educated can contribute to the cause. The most affluent and the poorest black American can make a difference.

All black Americans can be heroes of Project 2019 by taking the time to understand the movement, taking a stand by supporting the movement, and showing their faith by living the movement. All that is required is pride in the unique heritage of black Americans and the desire to pass this black pride on to our children, grandchildren, and all future generations of black Americans.

What Will Happen If Project 2019 Fails

Based on percentages of population, in 1996, seventy-eight percent more white Americans than black Americans graduated from college. One measurable objective of Project 2019 is to equalize the percentage of black Americans who earn college degrees versus the percentage of white Americans who earn college degrees. Of course, Project 2019 could be called a success if just one black American earned a college degree as a result of it. However, if in 2019, fifty percent more white Americans than black Americans are still graduating from college, Project 2019 can certainly be deemed a failure.

What will happen if Project 2019 fails? No one can accurately predict the future and even educated guesses are meaningless when assessing the future of a nation or an entire people. However, for those who choose to speculate, they should use history as one of their guides. By examining the past and objectively evaluating the present, it is possible to get a sense of what the future may hold.

If Project 2019 fails, race issues will continue to be some of the most contentious and divisive issues that

America will have to face. America will have to deal with these issues well into the twenty-first century. If Project 2019 fails, black America will continue to exist as a separate and distinct entity within America.

If Project 2019 fails, black America's status as a socioeconomic underclass will become more entrenched and perhaps even become permanently solidified. As a best case scenario, black America will continue to make modest gains over the next several decades and perhaps lose its underclass status before the end of the twenty-first century.

If Project 2019 fails, fairly or unfairly, white racists will quickly point out that black Americans were presented with the necessary information and the opportunity to succeed in America but chose to waste that opportunity. If Project 2019 fails, it will reinforce the belief of white racists that blacks are inherently inferior.

If Project 2019 fails, it could have a devastating effect on the psyche of black America. Black America would be forced to "take a look at the people in the mirror" and consider acknowledging the possibility that they can not overcome four hundred years of oppression except by a process of slow and painful evolution.

If Project 2019 fails, America will not be as free as it would have been if Project 2019 had succeeded. If Project 2019 fails, America will not be as strong as it would have been if Project 2019 had succeeded.

PROJECT 2019   ISSUE 23

What will happen if Project 2019 fails? While it is reasonable to disagree with predictions of gloom and doom and easy enough to make a case against any given negative impact, there can be no doubt that very little good can result from the failure of Project 2019. And, unfortunately, there will be no way around one harsh reality if Project 2019 fails. If Project 2019 fails, then, ultimately, black America will have also failed.

What Will Happen
If Project 2019 Succeeds

If in 2019, the percentage of black Americans who graduate from college is equal to the percentage of white Americans who graduate from college, then Project 2019 can be characterized as an unequivocal success. Project 2019 could be deemed a moderate success if, based on percentages of population, less than twenty-five percent more white Americans than black Americans graduate from college.

What will happen if Project 2019 succeeds? Again, one can only speculate and, again, history is probably the only useful guide.

If Project 2019 succeeds, race issues will rapidly lose their distinction as being some of the most contentious and divisive issues in America. Black America will rapidly lose its distinction as a separate entity within America and black Americans will begin to be regarded as just another ethnic group in America.

If Project 2019 succeeds, then black America's socioeconomic level will continue to rise until it equals or exceeds the socioeconomic level of the rest of America.

If Project 2019 succeeds, America will be a stronger and a better nation. America will benefit as a result of a better educated and therefore more productive populace. America's knowledge base will be increased as a result of the successful completion of Project 2019, giving America a better chance to meet the challenges of the twenty-first century.

If Project 2019 succeeds then black Americans will succeed. For the first time since blacks arrived in America, black Americans will be as educated as white Americans and black Americans will be as enlightened and as knowledgeable as white Americans. After four hundred years of Slavery and oppression, black Americans will finally have both the opportunity and the means to compete with the rest of America on fair and equal terms.

If Project 2019 succeeds, it will bring honor to all the heroes, black and white, who fought, suffered, and died so that black Americans could live in a just and equal society. If Project 2019 succeeds, it will bring honor and peace to millions of black men and black women who, for two and a half centuries, were born into Slavery and lived and died as slaves.

If Project 2019 succeeds, it will provide irrefutable proof of the resilience and the greatness of black America. The success of Project 2019 will serve as a positive legacy for all future generations of black Americans.

PROJECT 2019

HEROES

Project 2019 Heroes

Ultimately, there will be millions of Project 2019 Heroes. Listed below are some of the individuals who have contributed to the success of the movement.

Lucinda Acker   Robert & Annie Lee Allen
Robert & Mattie Allen

Gary Banks   Charles Bass
Matthew A. Beech   Sandra Bempah
Thelma Marie Bergman   Shirley Berry
Beverly Blount   DeEdra Bond
Diane Bond   Jenyce Bond
Tonoa Bond   Ervin & Loretta Booker
Marie Brown   Robert T. Bruce
John & Mary Bynum

Shirley Carney   Cheri Chatman
Vondell & Kimberly Clark   Barbara Cole
Joann Collins   Laurie Collins
Rev. William & Rose Collins

Eunice Daniels   Andrew Davis
Charles & Shirley Dickenson   Jeff Donaldson
Eric Dukes

Project 2019 Heroes

Leo & Ruby Eddings

Mary Gallimore
Arnold Giles
Mary Griffin

Herron Hall
Guy & Debra Harris
Thomas & Bessie Holman

Rev. Charles H. James
Tamicka James
Rosie Johnson
Altridge & Joyce Joiner
Paul & Rose Marie Judon

Reggie & Hiwote Lawrence
Taylor & Alma Lowery

Kily Malden
Camille Martin
Marjorie McCoy
Margaret Moore

Johnny & LaVada Napier

Benny & Doris Perry
Darrin & Kelly Polk
Victor & Lorene Polk

Ronald & Cathy Raspberry
A. Robinson

Barbara Franch

Parthenia Gardner
Calvin Giles

Nicole Hampton
Ron & Julia Henderson

Curtis James
Nina Johnson
Willie & Sue Johnson
John R. Jop

Andrew & Lois Love
Allen & Hazel Lyons

Paulette Malden
Wendell & Juanita Martin
Beverly J. Moore
Charles & Janice Murray

James & Karen Nelson

Henry & Stella Person
Kelcey Polk

Sallie Roache
Dan & Hinda Roseman

Project 2019 Heroes

William Saddler
Alf Sanford, Jr.
Bryan & Christina Sanford
Rose Sanford
Tina Sanford
Michele Small
Vera Staples

Angie Sanders
Alf Sanford, III
Felicia Sanford
Stuart & Kathy Sanford
Andy & Brenda Singleton
George & Hepsy Sosebee

Pamela Thornton

Artist Vinson

David & Kathy Welch
Charles & Rebecca Wilcher
George & Deborah Wilson

Charles & Bertha Wilcher
Dorothy Wilson
Sheila Woods

To my wife, Rose, my business partner and my friend: Thank you for your love and support.

Selected Bibliography

U.S. Department of Education. National Center for Education

Statistics (1997). Digest of Education Statistics 1996,

NCES 96-133, by Tomas D. Snyder. Production Manager,

Charlene M. Hoffman, Program Analyst, Claire M. Geddes.

Washington, DC: 1996

U.S. Department of Education. National Center for Education

Statistics. The Condition of Education 1996, NCES 96-

304, by Thomas M. Smith. Washington, DC U.S.

Government Printing Office, 1996

U. S. Bureau of the Census. Statistical Abstract of the United

States: 1996 (116th edition) Washington, DC, 1996

"Project 2019"
Book Order Form

POSTAL ORDERS: (Please Print)

Name: _____

Address: _____

City:_____ State:_____ Zip:_____

Price Each: $14.00   ($11.95 + $2.05 shipping/handling)

Mail completed form and Check or Money Order to:

Project 2019
P. O. Box 1096
Chicago, IL 60690

ON-LINE ORDERS: www.project2019.com

"Project 2019"
Book Order Form

POSTAL ORDERS: (Please Print)

Name: _____

Address: _____

City:_____ State:_____ Zip:_____

Price Each: $14.00 ($11.95 + $2.05 shipping/handling)

Mail completed form and Check or Money Order to:

Project 2019
P. O. Box 1096
Chicago, IL 60690

ON-LINE ORDERS: www.project2019.com

"Project 2019"
Book Order Form

POSTAL ORDERS: (Please Print)

Name: _____

Address: _____

City:_____ State:_____ Zip:_____

Price Each: $14.00   ($11.95 + $2.05 shipping/handling)

Mail completed form and Check or Money Order to:

Project 2019
P. O. Box 1096
Chicago, IL 60690

ON-LINE ORDERS: www.project2019.com